D1341858

M.G. CARS

Car Maintenance Series

M.G. CARS

A PRACTICAL GUIDE TO MAINTENANCE
AND REPAIR COVERING
MODELS FROM 1946

By

DAVID M. PALMER

With 126 illustrations

LONDON
C. ARTHUR PEARSON LIMITED
TOWER HOUSE, SOUTHAMPTON STREET
STRAND, W.C.2

PREFACE TO THE THIRD EDITION

This book, completely rewritten for the Third Edition, covers the maintenance of all M.G. cars introduced from November 1945. The range of models included in order of introduction is given in the list on page viii.

Maintenance information given in the book embraces both routine attention and overhaul, and will therefore satisfy the M.G. owner who does not wish to leave all maintenance work to others, and caters for the requirements of the more experienced mechanic and the professional repairer.

Many M.G. models have appeared during the period covered by the book, but the logical sub-division of the subject in the various chapters makes for easy reference.

The problem of encompassing all possible information covering the whole range of vehicles, including the front-wheel drive 1100, within a reasonable length has been difficult, but it has been made easier by similarity in design of engines and other components.

Grateful acknowledgement is made to the M.G. Car Co. Ltd., for their assistance in providing illustrations, and for permission to use the M.G. Trade Mark as a cover design, although the book is in no way a factory-sponsored production.

CONTENTS

LIST OF MODELS

Model	Date	Chassis Nos.	Type
Midget TC . .	1946–1949	0251 to 10252	Open sports 2-str.
1¼-litre Y . .	1947–1951	1885 to 7020	Saloon 4-door
Midget TD . .	1949–1954	0251 to 29916	Open sports 2-str.
1¼-litre YB . .	1952–1953	0251 to 1551	Saloon 4-door
Midget TF . .	1954–1955	501 to 10100	Open sports 2-str.
Magnette ZA .	1954–1956	501 to 18576	Saloon 4-door
MGA 1500 . .	1955–1959	10101 to 68850	Open sports 2-str
MGA Coupé .	1956–1959	10101 to 68850 (HM prefix)	Fixed roof coupé
Magnette ZB .	1956–1959	18577 to 37100	Saloon 4-door
MGA Twin Cam .	1958–1960	501 to 2611	Open sports 2-str.
MGA 1600 . .	1959–1961	68851 to 100351	Open sports 2-str.
Magnette Mark III	1959–1961	101 to 16776	Saloon 4-door
MGA 1600 Mark II	1961–1962	100352 to 109070	Open sports 2-str.
Midget Mark I . (948 c.c.)	1961–1962	101 to 16183	Open sports 2-str.
Magnette Mark IV	1961–onwards	16801 to —	Saloon 4-door
Midget Mark I . (1,098 c.c.)	1962–1964	16184 to 26787	Open sports 2-str.
MG 1100 . .	1962–onwards	101 to —	Saloon 4-door (front-wheel dr.)
Midget Mark II .	1964–onwards	25788 to —	Sports convertible
MGB 1800 . .	1962–onwards	101 to —	Open sports 2-str.
MGB 1800 GT .	1965–onwards	101 to —	Fixed roof coupé 2 plus 2

CHAPTER I

REGULAR AND SYSTEMATIC MAINTENANCE

As well as the trouble taken by manufacturers to make the design of their new vehicles as modern as possible, they have also taken great strides in the amount and method of servicing required by their cars. This can easily be proven by comparing a manufacturer's servicing schedule of, say, ten years ago with its present day counterpart; the two biggest variations are the number of jobs required at each service, and then the frequency of the servicing. Success in this 'ease of servicing' battle between the manufacturers means more sales appeal for their vehicles and the giant British Motor Corporation (of whom M.G. are a member company) have succeeded in their aim to cut motoring costs.

The cuts that were made to the servicing schedules about two years ago meant that instead of having to service his M.G. every 1,000 miles, an owner could go for a period of 3,000 miles between services, and even then the work that had to be carried out was less than the old original 3,000-mile service. The cuts were made possible by more efficient oils and better bearing materials being used, but it should be pointed out that now more than ever a vehicle requires its regular set services, for with the longer periods between one service missed would mean for the average motorist a six month gap between the attention it needs.

This means carrying out *all* the jobs on the servicing schedule at the correct times and includes using the right grade(s) of oils for the various major units—e.g. engine, gearbox, rear axle, steering box. It is false economy to miss out one or two of the harder jobs during a service thinking they can be left until next time, for before then trouble might develop.

All M.G. cars are supplied with Owner's Handbooks that

A*

give the full list of jobs to be carried out at each service and new copies of these books are still available for all post-war M.G. models if ordered through an official dealer; their price is 4/6d.

Although the new servicing schedules and periods were designed for current models, providing a car is in good condition, even if it is one of the earlier models covered by this book, it will probably perform satisfactorily being serviced at the new periods; but on the other hand, if the vehicle has worn ball races, joints, leaking seals and an engine burning oil, then it will need servicing more regularly to keep lubricant in these worn parts.

FIRST 500-MILE SERVICE

The first service a car gets once it is in the hands of its owner is at 500 miles and this is deemed so important that it is a free service for which the owner only has to pay for the materials used. It is the end of the 'settling-down' period and the car has to be given quite a thorough check to make sure that the units, assembled under mass production, have not developed any faults and are behaving as they should. Most important is the changing of the oils, as during the running-in period high-spots on the various bearing and gear surfaces will have worn down and there may be minute pieces of metal held in suspension in the original oil.

A 500-mile check generally consists of the following list of jobs:

1. Drain oil from engine, gearbox and rear axle (or power unit of front-wheel drive car) and refill with new oil.
2. Lubricate all grease nipples.
3. Tighten down the cylinder head and manifold nuts to correct torque figures.
4. Tighten rocker-shaft bracket nuts to correct torque figure.
5. Check rocker gaps and reset if necessary.
6. Tighten fan belt if required.
7. Check all water hoses and pipes for tightness.
8. Clean and reset carburetters.

9. Clean and adjust sparking plugs and contact points.
10. Check auto-advance/retard mechanism and reset ignition timing if required.
11. Check front-wheel alignment and steering joints.
12. Check tightness of propeller-shaft securing nuts and bolts (or drive shaft on front-wheel drive cars).
13. Check clutch-pedal clearance.
14. Check fluid level in clutch and brake master cylinders.
15. Test brakes and adjust or bleed if required.
16. Inspect operation of all electrical items.
17. Examine battery and top-up with distilled water if necessary.
18. Inspect shock absorbers.
19. Check tyre pressures.
20. Check doors for bad fitting, difficulty in operation, and lubricate their catches and hinges.

It is surprising during a 500-mile check, the number of things that do come to light, the most common being possibly incorrect setting of the ignition timing or carburetters due to the hurry at the factory to get the cars built, leaving no time for accurate setting. These things, and whatever else may be found, are therefore put right at a very early stage.

REGULAR PERIODIC MAINTENANCE

Services after this are now, as has already been said, at intervals of 3,000 miles, but of course it is not exactly the same list of jobs each time. The lists are set out below and cover a total mileage of 12,000, the services repeating themselves with this frequency. It will be seen that the work for a 3,000 mile service is only repeated at 9,000 miles; for 6,000 and 12,000 miles there are quite separate instructions and several different jobs to do.

Every 250 Miles or Once a Week
Check oil level in engine and top-up if required.
Check tyre pressures.
Check radiator water level (unless sealed system).

Every 3,000 Miles

Top-up carburetter piston dashpots.
Oil carburetter controls and cables.
Check fan-belt tension.
Check clutch master-cylinder fluid (hydraulic-operated clutches only).
Adjust brakes if necessary.
Check brake master-cylinder fluid level.
Inspect brake pipes for leaks.
Lubricate distributor drive-shaft and cam.
Clean air cleaner.
Check clutch clearance and adjust if required.
Oil door hinges, locks and bonnet locks.
Check level of distilled water in battery.
Change oil in engine (or power unit of front-wheel drive car) if standard SAE 30 or 40 oil is used.
Check levels in gearbox and rear axle.
Lubricate all grease nipples.
Change round road wheels, including spare.
Check tyre pressures.

Every 6,000 Miles

Top-up carburetter piston dashpots.
Oil carburetter controls and cables.
Check fan-belt tension.
Check valve-rocker clearances.
Lubricate distributor drive and cam.
Clean out air cleaner.
Clean and adjust sparking plugs.
Clean and adjust contact points.
Check clutch master-cylinder fluid level (hydraulic operated clutches only).
Check clutch clearance and adjust if necessary.
Adjust brakes if required.
Check brake master-cylinder fluid level.
Inspect brake pipe lines for leaks.
Check tightness of suspension and propeller-shaft (or drive-shaft) nuts.
Inspect brake disc pads for unequal wear (if applicable).

Oil door hinges, locks and bonnet lock.
Check level of distilled water in battery.
Check all lights and flashing indicators.
Lubricate dynamo bearing.
Change oil in engine (or power unit of front-wheel drive cars) if a Multigrade oil or normal SAE 30 or 40 oil is used.
Change gearbox and rear-axle oils.
Fit new oil-filter element.
Lubricate all grease nipples.
Change round road wheels, including spare.
Check tyre pressures.
Check front-wheel alignment.

Every 9,000 Miles
Repeat 3,000-mile Service.

Every 12,000 Miles
Remove carburetter dashpots, pistons; clean, reassemble and top-up.
Oil carburetter controls and cables.
Check fan-belt tension.
Check valve-rocker clearances.
Lubricate water pump sparingly.
Fit new air-cleaner element (if paper type used).
Lubricate distributor drive and cam.
Clean and adjust sparking plugs, fitting new ones if required.
Clean and adjust contact points.
Check clutch master-cylinder fluid (hydraulic-operated clutches only).
Check clutch clearance.
Check level of brake master-cylinder fluid.
Adjust brakes if required.
Inspect brake pipe lines for leaks.
Inspect brake disc pads for unequal wear (if applicable).
Check tightness of suspension and propeller-shaft (or drive-shaft) nuts.
Oil door hinges, locks and bonnet locks.
Check level of distilled water in battery.
Check all lights and flashing indicators.

Lubricate dynamo bearing.
Have headlamps beam set.
Change oil in engine or power unit.
Fit new oil-filter element.
Change oil in gearbox and rear axle.
Lubricate all grease nipples.
Repack front hubs with grease.
Lubricate steering rack or box.
Change round road wheels, including spare.
Check tyre pressures.
Check front-wheel alignment and adjust if necessary.

Lubricants

Only one of the recommended brands of oils should be used in the major components and B.M.C. Service give quite a choice for M.G. cars. For engines Esso, Mobiloil, Shell, Energol, Filtrate, Sternol, Duckhams, or Castrol oils of either the SAE 30/40 type or the multigrade varieties are allowed; if ordinary oil is used, the change point is every 3,000 miles, if a multigrade is used this only need be changed every 6,000 miles. Also, the multigrade oils *are* approved for the front-wheel drive M.G. 1100 which has a common power-unit oil for engine and transmission.

With gearboxes and rear axles make a check in the Owner's Handbook as to the correct grade of oil. Early models of the 1946/9 era were using SAE 90 oils in both these units, then with the advent of the front sliding-spline coupling for the propeller shaft, gearboxes had SAE 30 oils specified; rear axles all use a Hypoid oil of SAE 90 viscosity. With both these units, the brands of oils are as for the engine.

The servicing schedules given are open to variation depending upon the condition of the car, the owner's personal feelings on how often things should be done, and upon the usage the car gets. It will be noted that no set mileage has been quoted for decarbonisation and valve grinding and this is because it is impossible to gauge just when this work would be required, it differs from vehicle to vehicle. A general lack of power and rough running, coupled with high fuel consumption and an inability to tune the engine to run smoothly, will show when this work is required, but this could happen as early as 20,000 miles in some cases, or as late as 40,000 miles in others.

Pre-holiday Checks

Before commencing a motoring holiday or other lengthy tour it is a very good idea to give the car a check over to the extent of the 6,000-mile service jobs listed earlier; on top of this, inspection should be carried out on the steering joints and arms, wheel bearings, brake linings or pads, propeller-shaft joints for wear—the engine, gearbox and axle for leaks—and all nuts and bolts for tightness. It is much better to find any possible trouble spots and rectify them before the journey, for although there are B.M.C. Service depots able to deal with M.G. faults all over Europe, a breakdown spoils what could have been an enjoyable run.

Laying up the Car

Should the car be laid up for any length of time, it is preferable that it is placed on stands so that the weight of the vehicle is not on the one area of the tyres for this time. The radiator and cooling system should be drained as should the fuel tank and fuel system. Make sure the battery is disconnected, the car body is dry and clean, and that all grease nipples have been lubricated. Chrome and other bright metal parts can be treated with an anti-corrosive and occasionally the engine should be turned over by hand to keep it free from seizure.

CHAPTER II

ENGINE LUBRICATION SYSTEM

IN the previous chapter it was pointed out that only the maker's recommended oils should be used in the engines of M.G. cars, this is because there are now a great variety of makes on the market, not all of which come up to the standards set by B.M.C. Service. A number of engine parts are subject to very heavy loading during the running of the unit and it is therefore essential that the lubricant used is capable of forming the necessary film between the bearing surfaces.

Another important aspect is that oil also acts as a coolant, for it dissipates heat away from the bearings; but oils that are not suitable, or those of the wrong viscosity, cannot do this so well. Wherever possible keep to the grade of oil suggested for the engine.

There are two main types of oil pump used in the engines covered by this book, the gear type and the rotor type, and whilst they differ slightly in design they perform the same job although they go about it in a different way.

Gear-type Pump

This pump has as its heart two gears with straight-cut teeth running in mesh and situated inside a snug-fitting casing. One of the gears is driven by a shaft from the engine camshaft, the other being driven due to its engagement with the first. Inside the pump body, adjacent to the point of contact of the gears, are two openings; one is connected to the oil supply (the sump) and the other pushes the oil out under pressure to the main oil galleries.

As the gears rotate and the teeth become continually engaged and disengaged a vacuum is formed at the inlet port and oil is drawn in. It passes around the outside of the gears as they turn until it reaches the other side of where they mesh. At

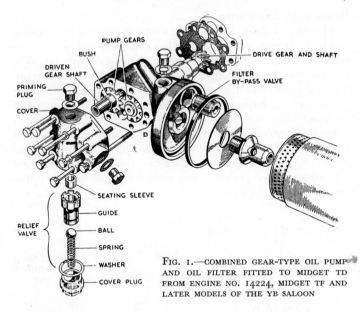

FIG. 1.—COMBINED GEAR-TYPE OIL PUMP
AND OIL FILTER FITTED TO MIDGET TD
FROM ENGINE NO. 14224, MIDGET TF AND
LATER MODELS OF THE YB SALOON

Note that on Midgets TC, TD (up to engine No. 14223), Y and early YB
Saloons, the pump and filter are separate units. On these models the
filter by-pass valve is mounted in the cylinder block above the oil pump; it
can be withdrawn by the use of a suitable 8 mm. stud and distance-piece.

this point, as each tooth runs into its respective trough, oil is
forced out of the exit port under pressure and into the main
system.

Checking Gear-type Pump for Wear

So long as the clearance between the gears and the outer
casing and the base plate remain within tolerance, this type of
pump will give an efficient output. If the pressure drops, the
pump can be removed for examination, the base plate removed
so that a straight-edge can be laid across and feeler gauges used
to measure the gap. This should not be more than 0·0035 in.
The clearance around the outer circumference of the gears and
the pump body should not exceed 0·0064 in.

Rotor-type Oil Pump

The biggest disadvantage of this type of pump is its situation inside the engine, for it is driven from the rear end of the camshaft and to gain access to the pump, the engine must be taken out and the clutch, flywheel and rear mounting plate taken off. The pump itself is made up of an alloy body and cover containing a large outer rotor with five internally-cut recesses and an inner rotor with four externally-formed teeth. The inner rotor is connected to the rear of the camshaft for its drive and the outer rotor is driven by the inner. The centre of the inner rotor is eccentric to the outer-rotor bore, so that whilst they are in contact at one point of their circumference, directly opposite they are far apart.

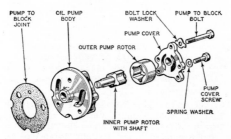

FIG. 2.—COMPONENTS OF HOBOURN EATON ROTOR-TYPE OIL PUMP

The tips of the inner-rotor teeth stay in contact with the outer-rotor recesses at all times, but as there are four teeth and five recesses, as the rotors turn a compartment is continually opening and closing. There are inlet and outlet ports in the pump body and as the compartment opens up adjacent to the inlet port a vacuum causes oil to be drawn in until the inlet port is closed off. As the rotor turns, the oil in this compartment is gradually squeezed out of the exit port, thus building up pressure in the lubricating system.

It has generally been found that the rotor-type pump gives no trouble at all until it wears out, and then all that can be done is fit a reconditioned unit. Due to the positioning of the pump, it is always wise to fit a reconditioned unit when the engine is out for overhaul.

Air in Lubricating System

It is vitally important that no air be allowed to get into the system on the suction side of the oil pump as this would stop oil being drawn into the pump body and an immediate pressure drop would result. With the gear type of pump, the body itself is generally submerged, or partially submerged, in the oil, but if not—as with the rotor pump—oil galleries on the suction side are kept as short as possible to obviate the risk of gasket failure causing a loss of pressure.

Controlling Oil Pressure

As oil is delivered under pressure to bearings with quite small working clearances, after the engine has run for a period of time this pressure will build-up beyond its safe limit. Should this not be controlled, the unusually high pressure could well burst a pipe or joint. The most common method of controlling oil pressure is by having a ball-valve with a predetermined spring behind it situated in the system. As the pressure builds up over the limit (which is generally between 50 and 75 lb./sq. in., depending upon the model), the ball is pushed off its seat against the spring pressure allowing oil to by-pass the system and return straight to the sump. An immediate pressure drop causes the ball to be pushed back on to its seat and the cycle commences again.

The pressure-relief valve is situated in the pump body itself (or cover) with the gear-type of pump, which is used mainly on the earlier cars, while with engines having a rotor-type pump, the valve is situated in the side of the cylinder block under a domed-hexagon plug.

Recommended oil pressures vary from model to model, but the oil pressure with engine idling is generally about 15 lb./sq. in and normal running about 55–60 lb./sq. in. If a pressure drop occurs, the first thing is always to try the pressure-relief valve, unless another cause is known to be present. All that can be done is to fit a new spring, ball, or plunger, and if the valve is of the plunger type it can have its seat re-cut with the special B.M.C. tool available for this job. There is no other adjustment to the oil pressure.

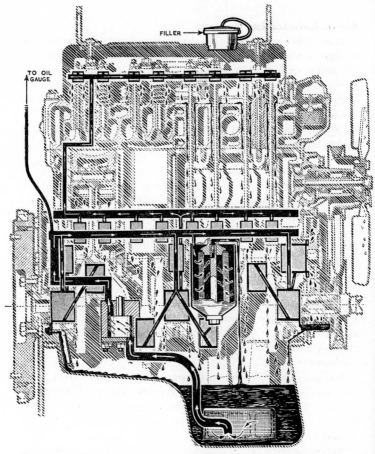

FILLER →

TO OIL
GAUGE

Fig. 3.—LUBRICATION SYSTEM OF THE B.M.C. 'B' SERIES ENGINE USED ON MAG-
NETTE ZA AND ZB

Causes of Low Oil Pressure

Other main causes of low oil pressure are as follows:

1. Air leak into induction side of pump.
2. Wear inside oil pump either on gears or rotors.
3. Gauze oil-pump strainer (if fitted) blocked due to dirty oil.

4. Worn engine bearings allowing oil to bleed away quickly.
5. Blocked oil-filter element.

Filtering the Oil

All engines have a gauze strainer in the sump itself, supplemented by an external full-flow or by-pass oil filter, the most common being the former.

With the full-flow filtering system, all oil to the main oil galleries must pass through the filter, and because of this a filter-relief valve must be fitted, for if the filter becomes choked the valve will be forced off its seat so that unfiltered oil can pass to the bearings.

With either of the two types of external filter, it can be seen that should the element become clogged then unfiltered oil gets through to the working surfaces; to avoid the scouring action that this would cause it is essential that the element is changed at the correct servicing period. The M.G. 1100 has no time limit, for a warning light on the fascia will stay on when the filter gets blocked.

Oil Pressure Warning

On the fascia of every M.G. there is either an oil-pressure gauge or a warning light that comes on should the pressure ever drop below the minimum allowed.

Twin Cam Engine

This high-performance engine has a more complex lubricating system because there are more components that require a pressure feed; as well as the crankshaft and camshaft bearings and the valve gear, the Twin Cam engine has to have oil distributed to a number of points in the timing cover.

The oil pump for this model is the rotor type which has already been described and the pressure-relief valve is under the domed nut on the rear left-hand side of the cylinder block. Idling oil pressure should be 10 lb./sq. in., and normal running about 50 lb./sq. in.

CHAPTER III

FUEL SYSTEM

B ECAUSE M.G. was one of the companies that formed the old Nuffield Organisation, and another member being the S.U. Carburetter Co. Ltd., fuel pumps and carburetters made by this firm are fitted to all M.G. cars.

S.U. Fuel Pump—Types L and HP

From 1946 up to the end of the fifties, the S.U. fuel pump changed little in design from its basic concept that dated to mid-way between the World Wars. The L-type is invariably mounted under the bonnet on the engine bulkhead, the HP in the boot of the car near to the tank; they are generally similar in construction.

The pump can be divided into three main assemblies: the contact breaker, the magnet assembly, and the diaphragm body—the latter being cast in two pieces with a gasket interposed between.

The magnet housing conceals an iron core (17), Fig. 4, surrounded by copper wire (18), which energises the magnet. Between the magnet housing and the armature (15) are fitted eleven brass rollers (10) which centrally locate the armature and allow freedom of movement longitudinally.

A small bakelite moulding carries the contact-breaker rockers (25) and (26), they being hinged to the moulding at one end and connected together at the other end by two small springs arranged to give a 'throw-over' action. A trunnion is fitted into the centre of the inner rocker and a bronze rod connected to the armature is screwed into this.

The larger of the two body castings has a filter (12) screwed into it, while the outlet union (1) is situated in the top of the body and the inlet union (29) at an angle to it.

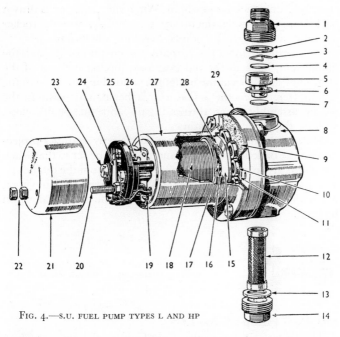

FIG. 4.—S.U. FUEL PUMP TYPES L AND HP

1. Outlet union.
2. Fibre washer (thick orange).
3. Spring clip.
4. Delivery valve disc.
5. Valve cage.
6. Fibre washer.
7. Suction-valve disc.
8. Pump body.
9. Diaphragm assembly.
10. Armature-guide rollers.
11. Retaining plate.
12. Filter.
13. Fibre washer (thick orange).
14. Filter plug.
15. Steel armature.
16. Push-rod.
17. Magnet iron core.
18. Magnet coil
19. Rocker hinge pin.
20. Terminal screw.
21. Cover.
22. Cover and terminal nuts.
23. Earth terminal screw.
24. Spring blade.
25. Inner rocker.
26. Outer rocker.
27. Magnet housing.
28. Volute spring.
29. Inlet union.

Pump Operation

When the pump is at rest, the contact points are closed and the electric current flows through the terminal, through the coil, back to the points and then to earth. This energises the magnet and attracts the armature, which as it moves draws the diaphragm back and causes a vacuum in the pumping chamber, thus sucking petrol in. When the armature is drawn back as far as possible, the bronze push rod operates the rocker assembly and opens the points, breaking the circuit.

The spring behind the armature then pushes it, and the diaphragm, back to the old positions, forcing fuel out of the pumping chamber via the outlet port and along the pipe to the carburetter. When the armature reaches its old position, the rocker assembly 'over throws' again and the points close, starting the cycle over again.

The spring blade of the contact points rests against a projection on the bakelite moulding and it should be set so that when the points are in contact it is deflected back from the moulding. The width of the points gap should be in the region of 0·030 in. when the rocker is pulled back against the face of the iron housing.

Fig. 5.—CORRECT SEQUENCE FOR ASSEMBLING COMPONENTS ON FUEL-PUMP TERMINAL SCREW

S.U. Fuel Pump—Type LCS

This pump is fitted to the Twin Cam model and the MGA 1600 and it functions in much the same way as the pumps described above. It is also similar in design, except that the formation of the body is different to give more advantageous pumping facilities. The inlet and outlet unions protrude from the body endwise instead of at right angles and the valve assemblies are accessible through the top cover, this being held in place by setscrews.

S.U. Fuel Pump—Type PD

Only one M.G. model used the ill-fated PD pump, this being the Magnette Mark III and, as can be seen from the accompanying diagram, this pump is considerably different to the older versions. In service, the PD pump was not very successful and it was soon replaced by the modified SP and AUF types. Only the parts shown exploded in the diagram can

Fig. 6 (*right*).—S.U. FUEL PUMP, TYPE PD

1. Top cover.
2. Filter.
3. Cork sealing disc for bottom dished cover.
4. Bottom dished cover.
5. Dished washer.
6. Spring washer.
7. Nut for dished cover.

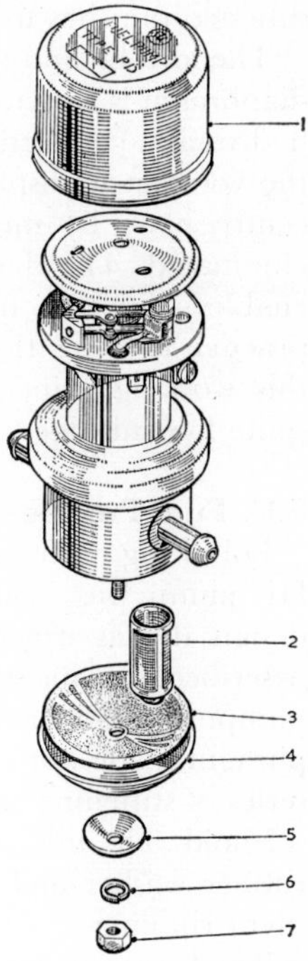

Fig. 7 (*below*).—S.U. FUEL PUMP TYPES SP AND AUF

1. Body.
2. Filter.
3. Nozzle inlet.
4. Washer for nozzle.
5. Outlet valve.
6. Inlet valve.
7. Valve retainer.
8. Screw for retainer.
9. Coil housing.
10. Tag (5 B.A. terminal).
11. Tag (2 B.A. terminal).
12. Earth screw.
13. Spring washer.
14. Housing to body screw.
15. Diaphragm assembly.
16. Spring.
17. Roller.
18. Rocker and blade.
19. Blade.
20. Tag (2 B.A. terminal).
21. Screw for blade.
22. Dished washer.
23. Spindle for contact breaker.
24. Pedestal.
25. Pedestal to housing screw.
26. Spring washer.
27. Screw for terminal.
28. Spring washer.
29. Lead washer for screw.
30. Nut for screw.
31. End cover.
32. Nut for cover.
33. Shakeproof washer.
34. Lucar connector.
35. Terminal knob.
36. Rubber sleeve.

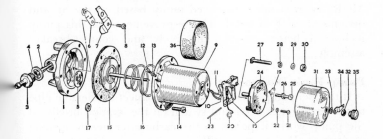

be worked upon; if trouble is suspected elsewhere, a reconditioned unit has to be purchased.

The idea behind the PD pump was very good in theory; the diaphragm is actuated magnetically through the medium of a hydrostatic connection, for with this the lost motion between the volumetric displacement of the pump diaphragm and its centre plate by mechanical means (as on early pumps) is eliminated. The diaphragm only flexes a small amount and enables Terelene film to be used for its construction. In practice it seems that not enough testing was carried out on this working principle, for the pumps failed consistently at quite low mileage.

S.U. Fuel Pumps—Types SP and AUF

Following on from the PD, an improved version of the old HP pump was brought into service and called the SP. In design it was exactly the same as the L and HP already described, having the same three main assemblies, but the pumping chamber was much smaller due to an improved diaphragm made out of two layers of neoprene and carried in a series of stiffening washers, the armature being operated by a solenoid. The inlet and outlet valves use Melinex film, and a rubber washer and spring are fitted to the armature to give silent running.

The SP pump can be fitted to models in place of the old PD, a conversion kit being available, and if the constant failure of the PD are costing a lot of money this is worth having done.

On the very latest models (Magnette IV, Midget, 1100 and MGB) an even more improved pump based on the SP and designated AUF is fitted. The improvements on this pump include a better main pump body and contact-breaker assembly.

Pump Fault Diagnosing

If the fuel pump ceases to work, disconnect the flexible pipe to the carburetter bowl and switch on the ignition briefly; if the pump works it points to the carburetter needle sticking on its seat. If the pump still does not work, disconnect the wire to the terminal and touch it against the metal of the body, when a spark should occur; if not then the wiring or battery is faulty.

Further checking gets more difficult on any models where the pump is situated in the boot or underneath, for the contact-breaker cover must be taken off so that the points can be checked. Clean them by inserting a piece of clean card, hold the points together, and slide the card back and forth a few times. If, when the terminal is replaced and the ignition switched on, the points fail to open, or are stuck open, there is an internal fault and a new unit is required.

A noisy pump is generally caused by an air leak into the suction side of the pump. Check all unions and joints, making sure the filter plug and inlet union are quite airtight. If necessary, the valves inside the two unions should be removed for cleaning, but always see the fibre washers are renewed and replaced exactly as they were.

One point while on the subject of noisy pumps is that the PD pump *does* continue to 'tick' even when the engine is not running, the ignition is switched on, and the carburettor full. There is nothing wrong with the pump if it does this and is otherwise working satisfactorily, and unless the ticking is extremely noisy there is no need to change the pump.

Reconditioned fuel pumps can be obtained from any B.M.C. Service garage, as can conversion kits to change later pumps such as PD to SP or AUF.

THE S.U. CARBURETTER

The S.U. carburetter is of the automatically variable-choke type, in which the size of the main air passage (or venturi) over the jet, and the effective area of the jet, are variable according to the degree of throttle opening used on the engine against the loading—which of course differs widely from light cruising to heavy pulling. A typical example of the S.U. carburetter is shown in Fig. 8.

The bottle-shaped dashpot, or suction chamber is mounted above the main carburetter body and houses a piston, the bottom part of which fits into the main body and blocks off the venturi. Under the piston and attached to it by means of a

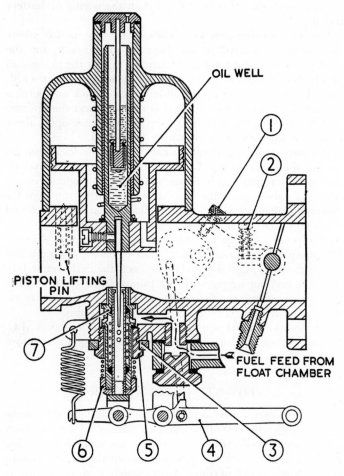

FIG. 8.—THE S.U. BASIC-TYPE CARBURETTER

1. Outer adjusting screw
2. Idling stop-screw.
3. Sealing cork.
4. Jet lever.
5. Locking-screw.
6. Jet-adjusting nut.
7. Jet gland.

clamp screw, is a taper needle that fits into the jet which is screwed into the underside of the main body.

When the piston is lifted, the air passage is enlarged and the taper needle is drawn out of the jet all in one movement. The space in the dashpot above the piston is connected to the inlet manifold by drillings in the piston body, thereby any depression in the manifold is felt on the topside of the piston and this vacuum lifts it in the dashpot. The further the throttle butterfly is opened, the greater the depression and the higher the piston will rise. This means more air enters the carburetter and as the taper needle moves up the jet, more fuel is allowed to flow out into the air stream and be carried into the engine.

Only one size jet is used in the majority of the carburetters used on M.G. cars, this being the 0·090 in. bore, but the larger choke carburetters have a 0·100 in. jet. The taper needles are available in a large variety of sizes, all offering different mixture characteristics and, therefore, it is possible to have a choice of three needles for many engines, giving standard, rich, and weak settings. At the end of this chapter a list of carburetter types fitted to the M.G. models covered by this book is given, together with the needles for each model.

Tuning Single S.U. Carburetter

Knowing that the jet and needle are correct, tuning is confined to correct idling adjustment, and this is carried out by turning the idling stop screw (2), Fig. 8, and the jet-adjusting nut (6), but before making these adjustments it is essential that the engine is at normal running temperature.

Set the idle stop screw to give a reasonably brisk tick-over (as this can be reduced later after setting the jet) and then the position of the jet can be adjusted so that the fastest idling speed consistent with even running is achieved. The mixture strength can be checked when it is thought to be correct by lifting the piston in the venturi about $\frac{1}{8}$ in. by means of the piston lifting pin shown in the diagram. Older carburetters may not have one of these, and then the piston must be lifted through the rear flange of the carburetter, after taking off the air cleaner, by means of a long thin screwdriver.

A guide to the correct mixture strength can be obtained

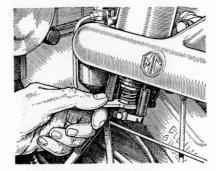

FIG. 9.—ALTERING THE POSI-
TION OF THE JET-ADJUSTING
NUT TO EITHER ENRICH OR
WEAKEN THE MIXTURE

This adjustment may
necessitate resetting the slow-
running.

from the exhaust and the movement of the engine; if the firing
is uneven and the engine rocks about, the exhaust colourless,
then the mixture is too weak and the jet adjusting nut (6) has
to be screwed down to enrich the mixture. If the engine has a
deep, rough misfire and the exhaust is black and sooty then the
mixture is too rich and the jet adjusting nut has to be screwed
up into the body to weaken it.

With the engine running evenly, the piston can be lifted
$\frac{1}{8}$ in. by the lifting pin; with the correct mixture strength, the
engine should be heard to accelerate minutely for a couple of
seconds and then settle down again. With too weak a mixture,
the engine will stall almost as soon as the piston is lifted; if too
rich, the engine will increase in revs and continue to do so for a
few seconds. Final perfect setting of the mixture can therefore

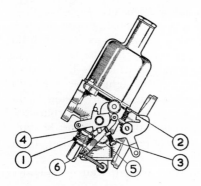

FIG. 10.—CARBURETTER AD-
JUSTMENT POINTS ON THE HS2
UNIT

1. Jet adjusting nut.
2. Throttle adjusting screw.
3. Fast-idle adjustment screw.
4. Jet locking nut.
5. Float-chamber bolt.
6. Jet link securing screw.

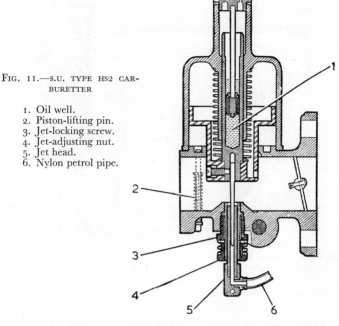

FIG. 11.—S.U. TYPE HS2 CAR-
BURETTER

1. Oil well.
2. Piston-lifting pin.
3. Jet-locking screw.
4. Jet-adjusting nut.
5. Jet head.
6. Nylon petrol pipe.

be made by careful manipulation of the jet-adjusting nut combined with regular checks by lifting the piston.

When the mixture is satisfactorily set, the idling stop screw
can be moved in or out to give the best tick-over speed for the
engine and driver. Should an air cleaner have to be removed to
set a carburetter, the jet-adjusting nut should be screwed in
one flat after replacing the cleaner to make up for the slight en-
richening of the mixture due to the blocking of the air passage
by the filter.

Tuning Multi-carburetter Layouts

To tune a multi-carburetter engine properly, the engine
itself must be in good condition, the plugs, points, tappets
clean and correctly set and the carburetters themselves with
clean dashpots and pistons, oil in the piston hollow rods, and
correctly centred jets.

FIG. 12.—INTERCONNECTING JOINT ON THROTTLE SPINDLE AND THE TWO SCREWS FOR SETTING IDLING SPEED ON TWIN-CARBURETTOR LAYOUTS EXCEPT LATEST MODELS

For latest models, see Fig. 13.

Commence the tuning by slackening the clamp bolts on the connections between the two carburetter throttle spindles so that the throttles can be set independently of each other; also disconnect the jet choke-control linkage from one of the carburetters. Take the two dashpots off and make sure that the needles are fitted into the bottom of each piston in exactly the same positions, and also that the jets are in approximately the same position on each of the main body jet bridges. A way of doing this is to screw each jet-adjusting nut right up into the body as far as it will go and then unscrew each nut a set amount—say, one full turn, or six flats on the hexagon, which is a good starting point for tuning.

Undo the throttle-adjusting screws (idling stop screws) and then turn each of them back until they just grip a thin strip of paper between the end of the screw and the piece of the main body that acts as a fixed stop—this means the throttle butterflys are completely shut, so screw each idling-stop screw in a complete turn and this will provide the basis for a tick-over.

Later models, such as the Midget (from 1961), both versions of the MGB and 1100, have different carburetter throttle-interconnecting linkage and the way to set this prior to tuning is as follows (see Fig. 13):

With the throttle-shaft levers free on the throttle-inter-connecting shaft, put a 0·012 in. feeler gauge between the throttle-shaft stop and the choke-control interconnecting rod. Move each throttle-shaft lever down in turn until the lever pin rests against the lower arm of the fork quite lightly. Tighten the clamp bolt on the throttle-shaft lever at this position and

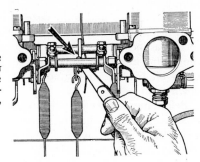

FIG. 13.—CHECKING THE 0·012 IN. CLEARANCE BETWEEN THROTTLE STOP ON TWIN HS2 AND HS4 CARBURETTER INSTAL-LATIONS—MIDGET (FROM 1961), 1100 AND MGB

when both carburetters have been dealt with remove the feeler gauge. The pins on the throttle-shaft levers should then have a clearance in their forks.

Matching the Throttle Openings

On all versions, it is now time to start the engine, the jets and throttles of both carburetters being set the same. Let the engine warm up to its normal running temperature and then, if necessary, the idling stop screws must be moved both by the same amount to give a suitable tick-over speed for setting the mixture—about 1,000 r.p.m. To perfectly match the throttle openings it is best to listen to the intake noise, after first removing the air cleaners.

This is most easily accomplished by holding one end of a piece of small-bore rubber tubing against the ear, while placing the other end against the flange at the intake of each carburetter in turn; the intensity of the hiss at each unit can be heard and the idle stop screws so adjusted to give the exact same noise from each carburetter, without moving too far away from the datum setting made earlier

Adjusting Mixture Strength

Once the throttle openings have been matched and the tick-over is correct, proceed to set the mixture strength at each carburetter.

As with the single-carburetter installation, the satisfactory running of the engine tells when this point has been reached; what has to be found is the fastest idling speed consistent with even firing. If, after moving the jet-adjusting nuts, the idling speed has increased from the datum setting and the running of the engine improved, then the idling-stop screws can be both eased off by the same amount to bring the tick-over speed down again.

Before moving the jet-adjusting nuts, remember that a weak mixture causes a 'splashy' irregular type of misfire and a colourless exhaust, whereas too rich a mixture gives rise to a 'thumpy' misfire and a blackish exhaust.

Check the mixture strength on each carburetter by lifting the piston about $\frac{1}{8}$ in. either with the piston lifting pin (if fitted) or through the back of the carburetter. If lifting the piston on one carburetter this amount stalls the engine, and the lifting of the other does not, then the mixture on the first carburetter is too weak. The correct mixture strength is when the lifting of the carburetter piston causes slight uneven firing due to weakness on the carburetter, but no stalling or acceleration of the engine.

Always make sure after any carburetter jet adjustments that the jet is hard up against the bottom face of the adjusting nut, and after carrying out the tuning do not forget to reconnect the choke control and interconnect the throttles again.

Although it has been described how the two jets are put in the same positions within their respective carburetters prior to the tuning, this is only to provide a datum setting to start the engine on; later, when the final mixture settings have been made it is very likely that the two jet-adjusting nuts will be in quite different respective positions in each of the carburetters. One might be two turns down and the other about two and a half turns down, but this discrepancy is well within the normal tolerance.

Even on new carburetters, the difference in jet positions when they are both tuned perfectly could be as much as one full turn of the adjusting nut, depending upon such factors as the position of the needle in the piston and the fitment of the gland-sealing washers, etc. On older carburetters, where there is also the factor of worn parts to influence the matter, the difference in position of the jet-adjusting nuts could well be as much as two full turns.

Centring the Jet

With the carburetter fully assembled, the dashpot piston should be able to be lifted the length of its stroke through the rear flange of the carburetter and when released be heard to fall back onto the jet bridge with a soft metallic click. If this does not happen, or if the movement of the piston is jerky and yet both piston and bore are known to be clean, then it is possible that the jet is slightly out of alignment. To overcome this problem proceed as follows:

Slacken the jet-locking screw under the body of the carburetter about one turn and disconnect the choke control from the bottom of the jet. Withdraw the jet from its assembly and take off the adjusting nut so that the spring behind this can be removed; replace the adjusting nut and jet, screwing the jet nut right up.

Remove the dashpot damper and press down on the top of the piston rod with a pencil; make sure the jet is right up to the adjusting nut under the carburetter, and tighten the jet-locking screw again. By holding the piston right down and the jet up, the thickest part of the needle is pushed into the jet, thereby holding it central while the locking screw is tightened. Finally, make the check of letting the piston drop down onto the bridge to hear the click.

Carburetter Maintenance

At intervals of 3,000 miles, the piston dashpot top should be removed, bringing with it the piston damper, and a thin oil of viscosity SAE 20 inserted until it fills the hollow piston rod. Do *not* fill to the top of the dashpot. At the same period, the external carburetter controls should be cleaned and the linkage for choke and throttles re-oiled.

Every 6,000 miles, the air cleaners should be removed and cleaned. The little wire-mesh filters can be cleaned in petrol and treated with a little fresh oil; with oil-bath air cleaners, dismantle, clean and replenish with oil to the correct level; and with paper-element filters, remove and blow clean with compressed air. The paper-element filter should be renewed at 12,000-mile intervals and at this time the carburetter dashpot and piston should be removed completely for cleaning.

Carburetter Faults and Remedies

Piston Sticking.—If the piston sticks in the dashpot there will be a noticeable drop in acceleration and a flat-spot will occur. The most common cause is simply dirt on the inside walls of the dashpot and a laquer-like substance on the piston side; if the dashpot and piston are cleaned at set periods this complaint will not occur.

A piston can also stick because of a bent needle or incorrectly centred jet, and this can be dealt with as described earlier.

Float Chamber Flooding.—If petrol runs from around the top of the float chamber and from the end of the feed pipe, it is generally caused by dirt in the float-chamber needle and seat. The float-chamber lid has to be removed so that the needle valve can be cleaned out. If the needle shows signs of wear around its seating, the complete valve assembly should be changed.

An incorrectly set float fork can also give rise to flooding. With the carburetters having a metal float, the fork should be set so that a $\frac{7}{16}$ in. ($\frac{5}{16}$ in. on early HS2 carburetters) round bar can be laid across the underside of the lid, and the prongs of the fork rest on this whilst the flat part is holding the needle valve shut. On latest HS2 and HS4 instruments, a nylon float attached to the fork is used, the check for this is carried out in the same way, but a bar having a diameter of $\frac{1}{8}$ in. should be used.

Float Needle Sticking.—If the engine cuts out for no apparent reason, the float needle may stick in the closed position and the lid should be taken off so that this can be inspected. Should the needle and seat be in order, switch the ignition on and off quickly while the lid is off, for if no fuel comes through it means the petrol pump is not working.

Effect of Altitude and Climatic Extremes

The standard tuning employs a jet needle broadly suitable for temperate climates and from sea level up to 3,000 ft.

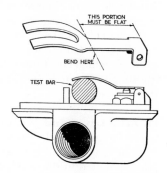

Fig. 14.—CHECKING FOR CORRECT SETTING OF THE FLOAT FORK

On the H1 carburetter, the test bar should be $\frac{7}{16}$ in. diameter, on the HS2 it should be $\frac{5}{16}$ in. and on the HS2 with nylon float only $\frac{1}{8}$ in. diameter.

Above that altitude, extreme climatic heat, or humidity may give rise to over-rich running and the necessary weakening of the mixture should take place.

If there is not enough adjustment on the jet nut to give a satisfactory mixture strength under these circumstances, then the owner will have to experiment with weaker needles until one is found that will suit the climatic conditions. Sometimes a weaker piston spring, or no piston spring at all will give the weaker mixture required without changing the needles.

S.U. DIAPHRAGM-JET
TYPE HD CARBURETTER

The HD carburetter differs from the others previously described insofar that the jet-assembly glands and seals are replaced by a flexible diaphragm and the idling is controlled by a metering screw located in the passageway in the carburetter body (17) Fig. 15, instead of by the throttle disc; the throttle jet interconnection is also modified. This carburetter gives more consistent idling, greater reliability of metering and reduced choke-control load. The HD carburetter is made in three sizes: 1½-in. bore, 1¾-in. bore, and 2-in. bore and can have either manual mixture enrichment or the cold starting attachment. The details of the carburetter are as follows:

The jet (1) which is fed through its lower end, is attached to a rubber diaphragm (2) by means of the jet cup and return spring cup, the centre of the diaphragm being compressed between these two parts. At its outer edge it is held between the diaphragm casing (5) and the float-chamber arm.

The jet (1) is controlled by means of the jet-return spring (6) and the jet-actuating lever (7), the latter having an adjusting screw (8) which constitutes the idling adjustment. Turning the adjusting screw in a clockwise direction, enriches the mixture and vice versa.

Throttle Lever and Jet Interconnection

The jet and throttle interconnection mechanism is operated by a cam (9) mounted on the jet-lever spindle (10), the whole being mounted in the diaphragm casing (5). The cam (9), on being rotated by the jet hand-control lever (11), actuates the cam shoe (12), thereby causing vertical movement of the push-rod (13), which is fitted with an adjustable screw (15), which makes contact with the throttle-stop lever (16).

It will be seen that angular movement of the jet hand-control lever (11) will turn the jet-lever spindle (10) and therefore, the jet actuating lever (7) which controls the jet cup (3) and the jet (1). The cam controls the cam shoe (12), push-rod (13), top plate (14) and the throttle. Suitable setting of the two adjustment screws (8) and (15) will clearly give any combination of mixture control and throttle opening.

Vacuum-controlled Ignition and Economiser Ports

The connection to the vacuum-ignition control and to the float-chamber vacuum-type economiser is made at the top of

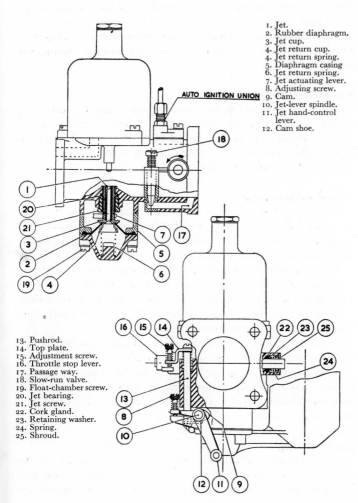

1. Jet.
2. Rubber diaphragm.
3. Jet cup.
4. Jet return cup.
4. Jet return spring.
5. Diaphragm casing
6. Jet return spring.
7. Jet actuating lever.
8. Adjusting screw.
9. Cam.
10. Jet-lever spindle.
11. Jet hand-control lever.
12. Cam shoe.

AUTO IGNITION UNION

13. Pushrod.
14. Top plate.
15. Adjustment screw.
16. Throttle stop lever.
17. Passage way.
18. Slow-run valve.
19. Float-chamber screw.
20. Jet bearing.
21. Jet screw.
22. Cork gland.
23. Retaining washer.
24. Spring.
25. Shroud.

FIG. 15.—JET AND CONTROL COMPONENTS OF S.U. HD CARBURETTER

the carburetter instead of underneath or at the side, as on the basic type.

This means that the throttle is opened downwards, assuming that the throttle lever is in the normal position, facing the intake.

Throttle-spindle Glands

Provision is made for the use of throttle-spindle glands, consisting of the cork gland itself (22), a dished retaining washer (23), a spring (24) and a shroud (25). This assembly should not require servicing and can only be removed by withdrawing the throttle spindle and disc.

Idling Adjustment

The HD carburetter still idles on the main jet, but the mixture, instead of passing under the throttle disc, is conducted along a passageway (17) connecting the choke space to the other side of the throttle disc.

The quantity of mixture passing through the passageway (17) and, therefore, the idling speed of the engine, is controlled by the slow-run valve (18), the quality of relative richness of the mixture being determined by the jet-adjusting screw (8), as mentioned earlier.

It follows that, when idling, once the engine has reached its running temperature, the throttle remains completely closed against the bore of the carburetter; for fast idling when the engine is cold, it continues to be partly open as with basic type, mixture passing through the passageway (17) and under the throttle disc.

Jet Centring

This operation is done in much the same way as for the basic type, described earlier, except that the float-chamber and jet casing must be removed and the jet held in the uppermost position by hand.

It is important to keep the diaphragm, and therefore, the jet in the same radial position in relation to the carburetter body and jet casing throughout this operation, as the jet orifice is not necessarily concentric with its outside diameter,

S.U. CARBURETTER DATA

Model	Type	Needles		
		Rich	*Standard*	*Weak*
Midget TC . . .	H2 Twin	EM	ES	AP
1¼-litre Y . . .	H2 Single	DK	F1	EF
Midget TD . . .	H2 Twin	EM	ES	AP
1¼-litre YB . . .	H2 Single	DK	F1	EF
Midget TF (1,250 and) 1,500 c.c. .	H4 Twin	H1	GJ	GL
Magnette ZA . .	H2 Twin	M	GM	GO
MGA 1500 . . .	H4 Twin	CC	GS	4
MGA Coupé . .	H4 Twin	CC	GS	4
Magnette ZB . .	H4 Twin	—	EQ	M5
MGA Twin Cam. .	H6 Twin	RH	OA6	OA7
MGA 1600 . . .	H4 Twin	RO	G	AO
Magnette Mark III .	HD4 Twin	FT	FU	FS
MGA 1600 Mark II .	H4 Twin	RO	G	AO
Midget Mk. I (948 c.c.)	HS2 Twin	V2	V3	GK
Magnette Mark IV .	HD4 Twin	FU	HB	FK
Midget Mk. I (1,098 c.c.)	HS2 Twin	M	GY	GG
1100	HS2 Twin	D6	D3	GV
Midget Mark II . .	HS2 Twin	H6	AN	GG
MGB 1800 . . .	HS4 Twin	6	MB or 5	21
MGB 1800 G.T. . .	HS4 Twin	6	MB or 5	21

Main jet, 0·090 in. (0·100 in. MGA Twin Cam).

and turning could cause decentralisation. The simplest way to do this is to mark one of the diaphragm holes and corresponding jet-casing screw hole with a soft pencil.

On the basic carburetter, the jet is controlled by a nut, but on the HD type it is set by screw (8). Also, whereas the engine speed on the basic type is determined by adjustment of the throttle, it is now controlled by the slow-run valve (18).

To enrich the mixture, the screw (8) should be screwed in, and to increase the idling speed, the slow-run (18) should be undone.

Defects in Operation

Since the HD carburetter is fed through its centre and has no glands, leakage can only be caused by an insecure fit of the jet cup, an imperfect seal of the diaphragm, either at its outer edge, or by facture of the diaphragm. Leakage at the outer edge or inner edge may be cured by tightening the float-chamber securing screws (19), but fracture or leakage at the inner edge will probably call for a new jet assembly.

The jet may also stick, either up or down due to dirt between it and its bearing (20), or due to corrosion. The cure is to remove the parts by undoing the jet screw (21), clean and refit.

CHAPTER IV

IGNITION SYSTEM

THE ignition-system layouts of all the M.G. cars covered by this book are very much the same, the main component parts being the battery, coil, distributor, sparking plugs, and ignition switch. The system consists of two circuits; primary and secondary, the primary being the low-tension side and the secondary the high-tension side.

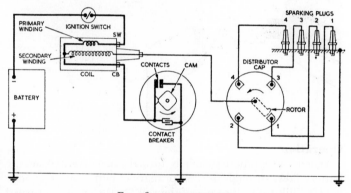

FIG. 16.—IGNITION SYSTEM

Diagram showing the two circuits in the system—the primary (or low-tension) circuit and the secondary (or high-tension) circuit. The low-tension circuit is indicated by the thicker line. Note four-cylinder 1, 3, 4, 2 firing order of the sparking plugs relative to the anti-clockwise direction of rotation of the cam and rotor.

On the coil, which is generally mounted on the bulkhead of the engine bay, are two terminals marked 'SW' and 'CB', while between them is a high-tension lead to the distributor cap. The ends of the primary-coil winding are attached to the terminals, while the coil secondary winding is attached to the 'CB' terminal only.

The distributor is situated on the side of all o.h.v. engines, the same side of the cylinder head as the sparking plugs, and incorporated in it is a means of automatically advancing or retarding the timing. Under the distributor cap is a base-plate assembly carrying the contact-breaker points, a cam which operates the points, and a rotor which fits on top of the cam. Inside the cap there are segments (either four or six depending upon the number of cylinders the engine has) to which are connected the sparking-plug leads, and in the centre a carbon brush which bears down onto the centre of the rotor. The ignition circuit diagram for a four-cylinder engine is shown in Fig. 16.

FIG. 17.—SETTING A SPARKING-PLUG GAP USING THE CHAMPION TOOL RECOMMENDED FOR THIS JOB

Operation

When the ignition switch is turned on, current from the battery flows through the coil primary circuit and a magnetic field is built-up in the core of the coil. As the engine is turned by the starter, the contact points are parted by the cam movement and the current flow is suddenly cut off. When this happens a very high voltage is induced in the secondary winding by the sudden collapse of the magnetic field.

This high-tension current is conveyed from the coil to the centre of the distributor cap via the high-tension lead. It runs down the carbon brush to the rotor and, depending upon which segment the rotor is passing, it flows through to one of the sparking plugs. This happens four times with every revolution of the distributor and each time the rotor is passing a different segment, therefore each plug in its correct turn is fed with high-tension current and a spark jumps the plug gap, igniting the mixture in the combustion chamber.

It can be seen from this description that the battery plays an important part, supplying current both for the coil and to turn the starter motor. It is therefore, vital that it is kept in good condition as described in Chapter XIV.

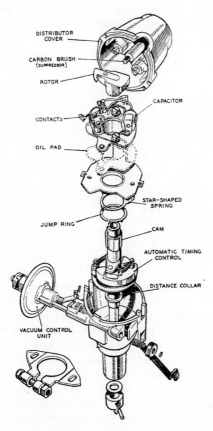

FIG. 18.—EXPLODED VIEW OF TYPICAL LUCAS DISTRIBUTOR

Ignition Maintenance

Every 6,000 miles, the sparking plugs should be removed, cleaned and reset, although in a worn engine that is burning oil this period could be as low as 2,000 miles. At intervals of 12,000 miles, the sparking plugs should be renewed.

Sparking plugs are made up of a centre electrode insulated from the outer case, which screws into the cylinder head and carries an outer electrode situated directly over the centre electrode so as to form a gap. When removing plugs for cleaning always use the correct type of spanner; the plugs can be cleaned with a wire brush, but better results are achieved using a proper plug-cleaning machine, and when setting the electrode gap (which is generally 0·025 in.) always move the outer electrode, never try to bend the centre one.

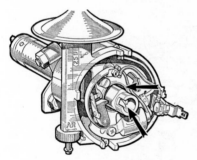

The knurled nut for accurate ignition timing is below the Advance and Retard mark AR. The contact-breaker securing screw can be seen just above the contact points.

Where arrowed, lubricate the cam spindle and the advance mechanism through the gap around the cam spindle. Also lightly smear the cam and moving-contact pivot pin with oil or grease.

FIG. 19.—LUCAS 25D-TYPE DISTRIBUTOR WITH CAP REMOVED

Distributor lubrication and contact-breaker gap setting should also be attended to at 6,000-mile intervals. The distributor can have its cap removed and the rotor taken from the top of the cam. A few drops of SAE 20 oil should be allowed to run into the centre of the cam spindle, while a few more drops applied to the outside of the spindle under the cam. A slight smear of grease should be applied to the cam faces.

To check the contact-breaker gap, the engine must be turned with the starting handle until the points are open their widest, then a feeler gauge of the specified thickness inserted between the points. If the points are dirty, or one has a build-

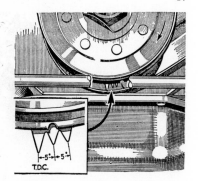

FIG. 20.—THE TIMING NOTCH ON THE REAR OF THE CRANKSHAFT PULLEY AND THE THREE POINTERS ON THE TIMING COVER THAT ENABLE TDC AND POSITIONS BEFORE IT TO BE ASCERTAINED

up on its surface, they should be removed, cleaned and replaced before checking the gap. This involves taking off the small nut and terminals from the spring end of the top contact and removing the screw, or screws (some early models have two) from the bottom contact. Be sure when withdrawing the contact points that it is noted how the fibre insulating washers between the contacts are fitted.

Each contact-point face can be cleaned on a piece of carborundum stone, keeping the face as flat as possible, then the contacts replaced, leaving the bottom contact screw(s) slightly slack. With the points still wide open, that is on the top of a cam peak, the bottom contact can be moved to bring the gap right, then the screws tightened. Do not forget the replace the rotor before putting the distributor cap back on.

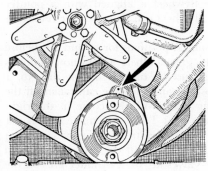

FIG. 21.—ON THE TWIN CAM THERE IS A SMALL PROJECTION ON THE TIMING COVER THAT HAS TO BE LINED-UP WITH THE NOTCH ON THE CRANKSHAFT PULLEY TO INDICATE TDC FOR NOS. 1 AND 4 PISTONS

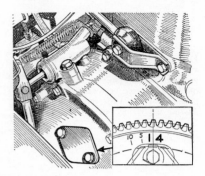

Fig. 22.—on the front-wheel drive 1100 a small plate has to be removed from the clutch housing before the timing marks can be seen

Ignition Timing

It has previously been mentioned how the high-tension current is fed to each sparking plug in turn, but the spark has to jump across the plug gap at exactly the right time; this being when the piston in that cylinder is approximately at top dead centre (T.D.C.) of its travel on the compression stroke. Therefore all engines have a pre-determined timing for the ignition, this figure being given in degrees of the crankshaft before top dead centre (B.T.D.C.).

The ignition timing for the various models is given in the Ignition Data table opposite.

When setting ignition timing, first bring No. 1 piston to T.D.C. on its *compression* stroke. A notch in the rear flange of the crankshaft pulley and a pointer on the timing cover when in line give this position—on the front-wheel-drive 1100 a $\frac{1}{4}$ mark on the rim of the flywheel is aligned with a pointer attached to the housing (flywheel can be seen after removing cover plate).

As well as the T.D.C. mark, positions for 5° and 10° before T.D.C. are also sometimes given. Where an ignition timing is 7° B.T.D.C., the engine must be turned so that the No. 1 piston is in its correct position and then the cap taken off the distributor. As the timing mark will also come in the right position when No. 4 piston is at T.D.C., to make sure No. 1 piston is at T.D.C. on the *compression* stroke, the valves on No. 4 cylinder should be looked at. Take off the rocker cover and turn the engine until the valves at No. 4 cylinder are 'on the

IGNITION DATA

Model	Champion Spark Plug	Plug Gap (in.)	Contact-breaker Gap (in.)	Ignition Timing
Midget TC . . .	L10S	0·021	0·011	T.D.C.
1¼-litre Y . . .	L10S	0·021	0·011	T.D.C.
Midget TD . . .	L10S	0·021	0·011	T.D.C.
Midget TD* . . .	NA8	0·021	0·015§	T.D.C.
1¼-litre YB . . .	L10S	0·021	0·015	T.D.C.
1¼-litre YB† . . .	N8B	0·021	0·015	T.D.C.
Midget TF . . .	NA8	0·021	0·015	T.D.C.
Magnette ZA . . .	N8B	0·020	0·015	8° B.T.D.C.
Magnette ZA‡ . . .	NA8	0·020	0·015	4° B.T.D.C.
MGA 1500 . . .	N5	0·025	0·015	7° B.T.D.C.
MGA Coupé . . .	N5	0·025	0·015	7° B.T.D.C.
Magnette ZB . . .	NA8	0·020	0·015	4° B.T.D.C.
MGA Twin Cam . .	N3	0·025	0·015	T.D.C.
MGA 1600 . . .	N5	0·025	0·015	7° B.T.D.C.
Magnette Mk. III . .	N5	0·025	0·015	5° B.T.D.C.
MGA 1600 Mk. II . .	N5	0·025	0·015	5° B.T.D.C.
Midget Mk. I (948 c.c.) .	N5	0·025	0·015	4° B.T.D.C.
Magnette Mk. IV . .	N5	0·025	0·015	4° B.T.D.C.
Midget Mk. I (1,098 c.c.) .	N5	0·025	0·015	5° B.T.D.C.
1100	N5	0·025	0·015	5° B.T.D.C.
Midget Mk. II . .	N5	0·025	0·015	5° B.T.D.C.
MGB 1800 . . .	N9Y	0·025	0·015	10° B.T.D.C.
MGB 1800 GT . .	N9Y	0·025	0·015	10° B.T.D.C.

* From engine No. 22735. † From engine No. 17994. ‡ From car No. ZA. 18101.

§ Lucas DKY4A distributor, Service No. 40162E with high-lift cams (used on later models).

Note following replacement spark-plug types for discontinued plugs—all set with 0·024–0·026 in. gap: L7 for L10S; N5 for NA8; N8 for N8B.

rock', i.e. one just opening and the other just closing. The timing mark should be almost exactly in place.

With the cap off the distributor examine the position of the rotor, for it should be opposite the segment in the cap for No. 1 plug lead and the contact points should be *just* beginning to open. If this is not the case, the distributor must be turned, after slackening the clamp if necessary, until the position above *is* reached.

On distributors having the vacuum advance and retard mechanism, there is a knurled nut that can be used for final accurate setting of the ignition timing. Before timing an engine, the nut should be screwed so that the scale is central in its housing, and then the setting made as detailed above. The knurled nut can then be used to either advance or retard the ignition a degree, or half degree, at a time until the best working setting is reached.

This final adjustment is best carried out when the engine is attached to an engine analyser such as a Crypton or Sun, as this type of equipment can time to the exact fraction of a degree. When altering the ignition timing using the knurled-nut adjuster, remember that each graduation on the scale represents $5°$ of timing movement and 55 clicks on the adjuster; therefore to advance or retard the ignition $1°$, the knurled nut must be turned in the required direction until it clicks 11 times.

CHAPTER V

ENGINE

Post-war models from the M.G. factory have, with one exception, only used two basic designs of engine—the 1,250 c.c. Nuffield unit from 1946 to 1955 and the B.M.C. 'B' Series unit from 1954 to date. The exception is the MGA Twin-Cam sports car which used an engine of very high potential but which, for a number of reasons, never quite fulfilled its early promise. In later years, the B.M.C. 'A' Series engine has been used to power the Midget (name reintroduced with model in 1961) and 1100, but this is merely a scaled down (948 c.c. or 1,098 c.c.) version of the 'B' Series unit.

The early Nuffield and the later B.M.C. engines are very similar and in the main can be dealt with as one. Both are four-cylinder overhead-valve engines with push-rods and rocker operation for the valves. There are detachable steel-bearing shells for the crankshaft journals and the camshaft runs directly in the cylinder block, or has one white-metal bearing; drive for the camshaft is by means of a roller chain etc.

This chapter can therefore deal jointly with these two main engines, and where differences occur they will be pointed out; the smaller 'A' Series engines are much the same except for their lubricating systems, but there is a special section set aside for the Twin-Cam unit as this requires some further explanation. The engine of the front-wheel drive M.G. 1100 is exactly the same as any other 'A' Series unit, the difference here comes with gaining access to the bottom half of the engine, for instead of a sump it carries the transmission attached directly to the crankcase.

Firstly, then, the details of the work that is common to all engines can be covered, regardless of their type and following this there will be specific information on the different types.

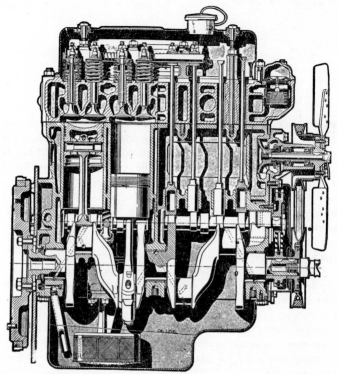

FIG. 23.—SECTIONAL VIEW OF B.M.C. 'B' SERIES ENGINE USED IN MAGNETTE AND MGA MODELS

Diagnosing Need for Top Overhaul

It is always very helpful to be able to diagnose accurately what fault there is with an engine, for nothing is more frustrating than to carry out a repair and find the old trouble is still present. With an engine there are two types of overhaul generally referred to in the trade as 'top overhaul' or decarbonisation, and 'complete overhaul'. The need for a top overhaul is indicated by a falling off in power, bad pinking when the engine is under load, and heavier than usual fuel consumption.

As the fall-off in power is gradual, the owner who uses his

car every day will probably not notice this until it gets very bad, but another check that can be made is turning the engine over with the starting handle. A four-cylinder engine should give four quite springy compressions over two complete revolutions of the handle; if there is very little resistance felt on one or more of the cylinders then it points to a badly seated valve and build-up of carbon inside the combustion chamber.

Diagnosing Need for Complete Overhaul

It is not necessary to completely overhaul an engine until many more pointers to wear become apparent; such things as loss or bad drop in oil pressure, knocks and taps from the engine bearings, slapping noises from the pistons, and heavy oil consumption. It is almost impossible to describe the differences between noises made by worn crankshaft bearings and other internal engine parts, for this kind of instant recognition of a noise only comes with practice and experience.

However, an engine in good condition should naturally be free from any kind of knock or tap when running, there should be no excess rattle from the timing chain, or badly noisy rockers. If there is any doubt as to the cause of an 'expensive' sounding noise in an engine, ask someone with experience to make a diagnosis for you.

Heavy oil consumption often indicates wear on the cylinder bores and pistons, but it must not be assumed that a healthy engine uses no oil; the opposite is the case, a normal unit should always use a certain amount of oil—probably about 800 or 900 miles to the pint—for this goes to prove all the necessary parts are receiving lubrication; on the Twin-Cam engine, the oil consumption is a good deal higher due to the increased working clearances. When consumption gets to around 200 miles per pint, or even 100 miles per pint if left that long, then it is fair indication that a complete overhaul is required. If the cylinders and pistons are worn to this extent, then the other components are in need of attention as well.

Oil Leakage

If the advent of heavy oil consumption is quite sudden then it points to a bad leak rather than any excess wear inside the

unit, especially if there are no noises from the engine and it is
still powerful. The leak can obviously be looked for under the
car, for the oil has to drop down onto the floor eventually,
but it is possible that the actual leak only occurs when the
engine is running, so to pin-point a leak of this nature check
the unit as it is running at a fast idle speed.

A faulty gasket or loose union, a cracked fibre washer or
badly fitted oil-filter element, can give rise to a considerable
oil loss, so do not immediately jump to the conclusion that
an overhaul is needed when consumption rises—look for leaks
first.

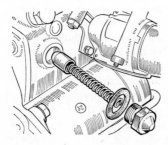

Fig. 24.—COMPONENT PARTS OF OIL-
PRESSURE RELIEF VALVE ON 'A' SERIES
ENGINE

It is situated on the side of the
cylinder block and a similar layout is
used on all engines where the valve is
not part of the oil pump.

Oil-pressure Gauge

This piece of fascia equipment is found on most M.G.
models as they have high-efficiency engines, but if one is not
fitted an oil-pressure warning light will be found mounted on
the fascia instead. Of course, the gauge is much more valuable,
for with the light the oil pressure can vary between about 15
and 50 lb./sq. in. and the light will remain out, leading the
owner to believe all is well; an accurate gauge, however, will
show up a low pressure as soon as it happens and could well be
the cause of having checks made that would entail only a small
repair, rather than leaving the wear until a complete overhaul is required.

On most M.G. engines, the tick-over oil pressure should be
at least 15 lb./sq. in. and the normal running pressure between
55 and 60 lb./sq. in.; the oil pumps are designed to give a
greater pressure than this, but a pressure-relief valve keeps it

down to the pre-determined level in the lubricating system. When bearings or journals begin to wear, the oil being delivered to them can escape more easily and a slight drop in pressure results. Attention at this stage can give the engine another lease of life quite cheaply, but if left the bearings will wear out completely, the crankshaft journals may be scored, and an overhaul is needed.

If the oil pressure drops and a knocking sound accompanies it then attention *must* be given to the engine immediately as it means that one bearing has for some reason worn out. Only inspection will tell whether this can be overcome by new bearing shells or a complete overhaul.

Symptoms of Bearing Wear

The drop in oil pressure and the knock from the engine invariably points to worn big-end bearings and if this can be detected before the unit starts to knock by watching the oil-pressure gauge it can save a lot of money.

With the main bearings in particular a little knowledge can make a big difference. The engine may appear to be running quite normally, only with a slightly lower oil pressure than usual, but if when running on a light throttle the pedal is suddenly depressed for maximum acceleration and a rumbling noise is heard, then slack main bearings are indicated.

There are pressure-lubricated moving parts which do not work under heavy loads, the camshaft and valve gear being instances, and when the bearings for these components begin to wear a certain loss of oil pressure will be noticed, but without any accompanying noises.

Timing Gear, Piston and Gudgeon-pin Noise

There are other knocks and taps that can develop in an engine, but which are not accompanied by a drop in oil pressure, these being piston slap, gudgeon-pin knock and timing-gear rattle.

Piston slap is more audible when an engine is started from cold and it gets less distinct as the unit warms up and expansion takes place on the aluminium pistons; sometimes—when wear is slight—the noise is not heard at all at normal running temperatures. As the wear gets worse so the noise will last longer and it will be most pronounced when the engine is pulling hard, but it will disappear on the over-run.

Gudgeon-pin knock is a light noise and can be diagnosed by shorting out the plug leads one at a time; when the knock goes, or diminishes, on shorting out a plug it points to the wear being on the gudgeon pin in that piston.

Timing-gear rattle is heard much louder from the front of the car (or the near-side front-wing area of front-wheel-drive model) and is clearer at low speeds. The valve timing on most models is by roller chains and sprockets, and the noise is set up when there is combined wear on the chain links and sprocket teeth.

Valve-gear Noise

The most common noise from the valve gear is a light tapping which indicates too wide a gap at the rockers. If these are set correctly and there is still noise it means wear on the rocker shaft or the rockers themselves. Of course, any valve-gear noise is heard at half engine speed and does not alter in frequency with engine revs.

Make Sure of Troubles

The effects and symptoms of heavy oil consumption have been covered and also the causes of various noises, but a warning must be given to prevent the owner who is not sure from commencing something which is not really necessary. Heavy oil consumption could be due to oil passing the valve-stem oil-seal rubbers, but if this is not the case, and the exhaust is very blue and smokey, then it is caused by wear on the bores and pistons. It will also be aggravated by wear on big-end bearings, for the oil escaping more easily from these means that it gets thrown up the cylinder bores in such quantities that the oil-control rings cannot cope with it.

With engines that have covered a large mileage and burn a lot of oil it is rarely sufficient only to true-up the bores and fit new piston rings—the crankshaft, big-end bearings, timing gear, oil pump and camshaft also have to be attended to, for it is just uneconomic to remove an engine and only partially overhaul it, when in a few months it will have to come out again for the jobs that were not done the first time.

It is this fact that has made the manufacturer's reconditioned engine schemes so popular, for as well as the time-saving factor involved and the ease in which the job can be carried out, an owner can be sure the unit has been *completely* overhauled, and he gets a factory warranty with the unit in case there are any settling-down troubles.

TOP OVERHAUL

The name 'Top Overhaul' refers to the decarbonising of the cylinder head and the cleaning and re-seating of the valves. When an owner decides to carry out this work himself, there are certain basic procedures that he must follow to succeed. These procedures are now explained and they refer to all engines used by the cars in this book, except the Twin-Cam which as will be seen from its special section has several differences. More specific detail on Nuffield, B.M.C. 'A' and 'B' Series engines will be found later in the Chapter under the relevant headings.

Cylinder Head Removal

Any job which involves splitting the main component parts of the engine means that the cooling system has to be drained and the top hose removed. The rocker cover and valve gear has to be taken off then the cylinder-head nuts can be slackened a little at a time to avoid distortion. When these nuts are replaced after the work has been carried out, it is important they are tightened in the correct sequence and to the correct torque figure.

With the cylinder-head nuts slack, the manifolds have to be removed after first detaching the exhaust system, but the carburetters can remain on the inlet manifold if there is room to withdraw the complete assembly from the studs on the head. The cylinder-head nuts can be removed and the cylinder-head lifted off its studs and placed on the bench. Keep the push-rods in their correct sequence for re-fitting.

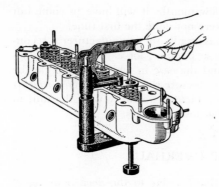

Fig. 25.—REMOVING VALVE-
SPRING COTTERS WHILE
HOLDING SPRING COMPRESSED
WITH SPECIAL TOOL

Decarbonising Piston Crown

It is not necessary to remove the cylinder-head studs before cleaning the top of the block with paraffin. Then turn the engine to bring two of the pistons to the T.D.C. position. Before scraping the top of the pistons to remove the carbon—a blunt screwdriver with a broad head being best for this operation—fit an old piston ring into the top of the bore so that a ring of carbon is left around the outer circumference of the piston crown; this acts as a valuable oil seal.

Be careful when cleaning the pistons not to gouge the soft metal, for this will help the formation of carbon after assembly and when the engine has run for a short time. With all the piston crowns clean and washed, wipe out the bores to get them clean as well, then apply a squirt of oil to each bore wall.

Valve Removal

A valve-spring compressor is required to extract the valves. This tool bears on to the head of the valve, while its forked end hooks around the bottom of the valve spring and compresses it so that the securing cotters can be removed. The compressor is then released and the valve spring can be lifted off the valve stem. Keep the springs lined up in their order of fitting so that they are replaced to the same valve. With all the springs off, the valves can be removed from the combustion chambers, again keeping them in numerical order on the bench.

Decarbonising Cylinder Head

If the combustion chambers are badly carboned, use a screwdriver to clean off any large chunks of carbon, then an electric drill with a wire brush attachment to take off the remainder and polish the surfaces. If no drill is available, clean off as much carbon as possible by hand, finally polishing with an emery cloth.

Always be very careful not to scrape across the valve seatings and try not to let particles of carbon enter the water jacket.

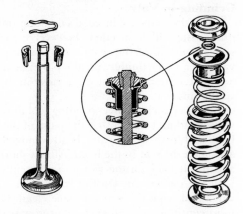

Fig. 26.—CORRECT METHOD OF FITTING VALVE-STEM SHROUD AND OIL-SEAL RING TO VALVE STEM ON 'B' SERIES ENGINES

Valves, Guides and Seats

The valves can now be inspected and any which have badly worn stems or burnt heads must be discarded. Those which are still serviceable can be cleaned, again using a wire brush and emery cloth. If a valve face is badly pitted it will take hours to grind out and it is worth taking any such valves along to your local repairer so that the faces can be re-cut on a grinding machine.

Any valve seats in the cylinder head that are badly pitted should be re-faced by means of a valve-seat cutter, this tool being one of a series supplied by the manufacturer for his various engines and have the correct angle for the seat. If this action is necessary it is important that any worn valve guides are renewed first, because the valve-seat cutter pilot fits through the guide.

Valve guides can be drifted out and in of the cylinder head using a bronze drift of the correct proportions, making sure that the guides are fitted back in exactly the same position occupied by the old ones. Measure their height above the cylinder head to the nearest $\frac{1}{16}$ in. and be accurate in the fitting.

With the valves, guides and seats all in good condition, the grinding-in process can commence.

Grinding-in Valves

Once the seats are in good condition only a fine carborundum paste will be needed; however if some pits can still be seen in certain of the seats use a coarse paste first. Coat the valve-head seat thinly with the paste, being careful not to get any on the stem, and place the valve in the guide with a light spring under its head.

A rubber-sucker valve-grinding tool must be attached to the valve head and then, using the palm of the hands, roll the tool back and forth so the valve head is moved with a semi-rotary action on the seat in the head. After a short time, lift the valve and put it back on the seat in a different position, continuing with the movement. Do this several times, then take out the valve and wipe the seat and face clean. Grinding each valve must continue until an even, matt-grey seating can be seen on both face and seat, with no pits or other marks present.

After grinding-in, thoroughly wash the valve, seat and guide with paraffin to remove all traces of abrasive, for if any is left it will very soon wear the stems and guides. The grinding-in process can be carried out quite easily with the cylinder head on the bench, but make sure it is placed so that each valve can fall freely on its seat and not come up against something that holds it slightly off.

Reassembling Valve Gear

Having progressed thus far, the valves now have to be replaced in the cylinder head. Where valve springs were removed and kept in order, make sure they are fitted back in the same positions and the right way round in certain cases—i.e. where there are close coils at one end they always fit against

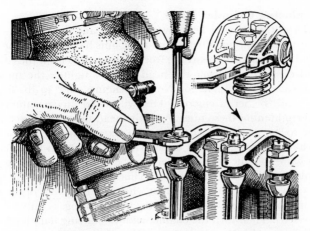

FIG. 27.—VALVE-CLEARANCE ADJUSTMENT

When the locknut is released, the valve clearance can be set by rotating the adjusting screw with the screwdriver and setting the clearance by means of a feeler gauge as shown in the inset.

the head. The spring also has to fit properly into the recess cut for it in the cylinder head.

With the spring fitted over the valve stem, the spring cup in place, the valve-stem sealing-rubber rings correctly in place (where used), the spring compressor is used so that the two cotters can be put into position and held there while the spring is slowly released. Watch each spring as it is let off, for sometimes one cotter gets displaced and the procedure has to start again.

Fitting Cylinder-head Gasket

Always use a new cylinder-head gasket. No jointing compound is required, but the gasket can be coated thinly on both sides with normal chassis grease to facilitate removal at some later date.

A gasket that can be fitted the wrong way around is generally marked 'Top' and 'Front' so that no mistake can be made. Locate the gasket accurately over the studs and press it lightly and evenly into place.

Replacing Cylinder Head

Drop the cylinder head over the studs and fit the nuts—the main thing to remember is that these nuts have to be tightened gradually and progressively, working outwards from the centre and criss-crossing over the head. Finally tighten the nuts to a torque of 50 lb.–ft. for Nuffield engines and 40 lb.–ft. for 'A' and 'B' Series engines. This will avoid any possibility of overtightening these nuts. With the head tightened down and the rocker gear in place, the valve-rocker clearance can be set.

Each rocker gap must be set with the tappet on the back of its cam and the setting order can be found by following the 'rule of nine' in the case of four-cylinder engines. For example, No. 1 valve can have its gap set when No. 8 valve is open (this being ascertained by seeing its valve spring is fully compressed). Then turn the engine with the starting handle; No. 2 can be set with No. 7 valve open, No. 3 set with No. 6 open etc., each case the sum of the two valves in question must add up to nine.

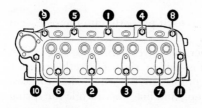

FIG. 28.—CORRECT SEQUENCE OF TIGHTENING CYLINDER-HEAD NUTS ON 'B' SERIES ENGINE

Completing Assembly

The remainder of the engine components can now be refitted, all cables and wires connected, and the engine topped up with water. With everything rebuilt, the engine can be started and run for a short time to get warm. The cylinder-head nuts must then be tightened down again and the rocker gaps reset.

After about 500 miles, the cylinder head nuts should be tightened again and all the rocker clearances finally checked to allow for any settling down that may have occurred. It is also a good idea to change the engine oil and filter in case any pieces of carbon have got into the lubricating system.

COMPLETE OVERHAUL

With a worn engine that is in need of a complete overhaul an owner must always consider whether he has the skill and facilities to carry out such a big operation, for it might be as well to make use of the manufacturer's reconditioning service. However, if it is decided to proceed, as with the top overhaul, there are certain jobs involved that are common to all engines and these will be dealt with first.

Engine Removal

Except with the smaller engines, where perhaps two strong men can lift an engine in and out, suitable lifting tackle with a capacity of at least 5 cwt. is required, together with a beam in the garage strong enough to support it.

With the lifting problem overcome, engine removal involves the taking off of the bonnet and radiator, disconnection of all cables, wires, hoses and other connections to the unit, and the detaching of the exhaust system. The engine front mountings must be undone and the clutch-housing bolts removed. A support should be placed under the gearbox. The engine can be drawn forward off the first-motion shaft and lifted out of the engine compartment.

On the front-wheel drive M.G. 1100, the complete power unit can be lifted out in a similar way, after all connections have been severed, or the front of the car can be lifted off the complete sub-frame, including suspension, brakes and wheels. Any work on the engine itself will entail the splitting of the transmission from the engine by undoing the nuts around the bottom of the crankcase.

If a reconditioned unit is to be fitted all that then need be done is for the engine bay to be cleaned out and the replacement installed. Of course, the carburetter, distributor, dynamo, starter etc. should all be inspected and also overhauled if necessary.

Cylinder Rebore and Crankshaft Grinding

It is practically certain that no owner will possess the boring bar and grinding equipment to carry out this work himself and therefore all that need be discussed here is the specification the owner has to give the machine shop who is to do the job.

With cylinder reboring, the machine shop should be allowed to supply the new pistons, then there can be no mistake over the sizes. The machinist will measure the bore wear and suggest the proper oversize, bearing in mind the manufacturer's set limits, i.e. up to plus 0·040 in.

A reground crankshaft should also be returned to the owner complete with the sets of main and big-end bearing shells in the correct undersize. It is a good idea to specify to the machine shop that when they supply new pistons and bearing shells that you want genuine B.M.C. parts and none other.

Bearing Replacement

When a crankshaft does not require regrinding during overhaul it is still necessary to renew the bearing shells, for even though the old ones show no sign of breaking up, their diametrical clearance is more than it should be. Never try to take up this wear by filing the ends of the shell bearings, for they are made to a perfect circle and if anything is done to change this very quick crankshaft journal wear will result.

If the crankshaft is still standard in its journal size, new sets of main and big-end shells can be obtained from B.M.C. Service dealers and fitted. The shells have small abutments at their rear that fit into cuts in the connecting-rod and main-bearing housings, thereby making it easy to fit the shells correctly. Always make absolutely sure these locating tags are correctly aligned before tightening the bearing caps.

Prior to the fitting of new bearings, and certainly after receiving a reground crankshaft back from the machine shop, make sure that its oil-ways are clean. This is best achieved by blowing through each hole with a compressed air line, but if this is not possible wash the crankshaft with petrol and use a tyre pump on the oil holes to blow them clean.

Rear Main-bearing Oil Thrower

Certain of the engines, including those used on the Midgets, have an oil-return thread on the rear end of the crankshaft behind the main bearing to stop oil getting past and into the

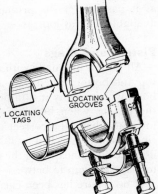

FIG. 29.—BIG-END BEARING SHELLS, SHOWING THEIR LOCATING TAGS AND THE GROOVES IN THE CONNECTING ROD AND CAP THAT THEY MUST FIT IN

clutch housing. This is very effective providing it is set-up properly.

The housing for the oil thrower is integral with the rear main-bearing cap at the bottom and cannot therefore be adjusted, but the top half is attached to the rear of the cylinder block by means of three bolts and there has to be a radial clearance of *exactly* 0·004 in. between the oil-thrower thread and its housing. Any excess clearance or eccentricity will make the oil thrower act as a pump and push oil out into the clutch.

Normally, no wear takes place on the parts of the oil thrower because nothing is in contact, but with the engine dismantled the thread must be inspected and cleaned out; the main bearing cap and top half of the housing examined and if any imperfections are found renewed. The importance of the oil thrower again emphasises the fact that nothing should be done to the shell bearings to alter their size, otherwise it will be impossible to obtain the correct running clearance around the thread.

The front-wheel drive M.G. 1100 has a plain rear main-bearing cap, the oil being stopped from reaching the clutch by means of a plug in the end of the crankshaft oilway and an oil seal that fits over the primary gear and prevents oil from getting beyond the flywheel housing. Great care must be

C

taken when fitting this seal to make sure its lip is not damaged as it passes over the primary-gear splines. A special tool is available for this job.

Pistons and Rings

All pistons are made with a pre-determined clearance at the top and bottom when they are fitted to a correctly machined bore, which is why it is important for the machinist to supply the pistons when he rebores the cylinder. The piston rings must also have the correct gap between their ends and each ring has to be checked by taking it off the piston and inserting it in the bore, measuring the gap and if necessary filing one end to bring the gap to between 0·007 and 0·013 in.

If no rebore has been carried out, but merely the fitting of new compression or oil-control rings, the same ring gap applies. With pistons having split skirts, when they are taken to be fitted with new or oil-control rings it is a good idea to have the pistons koetherised. This means the bottom of the skirt is expanded slightly to make it a closer fit in the bore. Pistons have to be sent to a recognised piston stockist for this treatment

NUFFIELD 1,250 c.c. ENGINE

This engine is fitted to the Midget TC, TD, and early TF and also to the 1¼-litre Saloon and Tourer Y and Saloon YB (year range 1946–54).

A 1,466 c.c. version of this engine (achieved by enlarging the cylinder bores), was fitted in Nov. 1954 to the Midget TF until its termination in April 1955.

Sump Removal

With the TC and saloon models this is quite simple, all that need be done is for the drain plug—situated on the nearside of the sump—to be removed to drain the oil and then the sump-securing bolts withdrawn. Take out the steering-drag link and the sump will drop down.

On TD and early TF models, the front of the car has to be jacked up, then the oil drained and the dipstick removed. Take off the exhaust system and release the clutch pedal pull-off spring, withdraw the split-pin and clutch pin holding the intermediate clutch-operating lever to the operating rod. Remove the two bolts holding the clutch-abutment bracket to the sump, take out the split-pin and take off the intermediate-operating lever. The sump can be lowered after removing its securing bolts. The fixture for the engine fume pipe is attached to the first bolt below the crankcase and sump-joint line on the nearside of the flywheel housing.

Always for the sake of peace of mind fit a new sump gasket when replacing the sump, and use jointing compound on it if you wish, although this makes it a much harder job to clean off next time the sump is removed.

Cylinder Head

To remove the head, disconnect the battery and the sparking-plug leads, drain off the coolant and remove the bonnet and sparking plugs. Disconnect the throttle, choke and petrol connections to the carburetter then take the carburetters off the manifold and both manifolds off the cylinder head. Disconnect the top radiator hose and remove the rocker-gear oil-feed line, fume pipe, and side cover. Take off the rocker cover, remove the rocker assembly and push-rods, remove the remainder of the cylinder-head nuts and the head can be lifted off its studs.

Valve Timing and Clearances

Top dead centre position can be found by turning the engine on the starting handle until the notch on the crankshaft pulley lines up with the pointer on the timing-chain cover. Cylinders No. 1 and 4 will then be at T.D.C. (see also Chapter IV). The timing chain is endless and has two bright links marked with a T. For correct valve timing these links must be fitted over the sprocket teeth similarly marked T, then the crankshaft and camshaft turned so that their Woodruff keys come in the right position for the two sprockets to be pushed on.

To set the valve-rocker gaps, slacken the locknut on each rocker and turn adjusting screw until the correct gap of 0·019 in. is obtained between the end of the rocker and the top of the valve stem. The locknut must be tightened when this gap is correct. For the setting procedure, see under Replacing Cylinder Head, earlier in this chapter.

B.M.C. 'A' SERIES ENGINE

This unit is the smallest of the current B.M.C. o.h.v. push-rod engines and is fitted to the new model Midgets (model name reintroduced in 1961) and the 1100 front-wheel drive car.

Removing the Sump

Midget Models.—The sump can easily be removed by first draining the oil and then undoing the fourteen bolts and spring washers that secure it to the cylinder block. This exposes the oil-pump pick-up filter that is attached to the two rearmost main-bearing caps by bolts and spring washers (early models only).

1100 Model.—With the 1100 there is no sump, the transmission being attached to the underside of the engine in its place. Any work that has to be done on the bottom half of the engine necessitates the complete removal of the power unit so that it can be split into its two separate units. This operation has been covered earlier in the chapter.

Cylinder Head

This can be removed as follows: take off the bonnet and drain the cooling system. Disconnect the battery and the top radiator hose, remove the air cleaners, and disconnect the throttle, choke, and fuel lines to the carburetters. Disconnect the heater hose from the rear of the cylinder head (if heater is fitted) and take off the sparking-plug leads and remove the plugs.

Detach the carburetters from the inlet manifold and then remove both manifolds from the engine, remembering to disconnect the pipe before trying to take off the exhaust one. Remove the valve-rocker cover and gradually slacken the cylinder-head nuts; the rocker-gear nuts (of which some also secure the cylinder head) can then be taken off completely and the rocker assembly removed. When removing the rocker

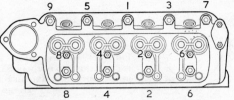

9 5 1 3 7

Fig. 30.—CORRECT
SEQUENCE OF TIGHT-
ENING CYLINDER-
HEAD NUTS ON 'A'
SERIES ENGINE

assembly it will be seen that the front right-hand stud has a
special lockwasher, as have all the subsequent studs down this
side. Do not lose these or replace them with ordinary washers.

The push-rods can now be taken out and stored in their
correct order, the rest of the cylinder-head nuts undone, and
the head lifted off its studs and placed on the bench.

Oil Pump

Unlike the earlier Nuffield engine with its gear-type oil
pump, the 'A' Series engine uses a rotor-type pump and this
is situated at the rear end of the camshaft, being driven
directly from it. Therefore, to gain access to the pump the
complete engine has to be removed from the car so that the
clutch, flywheel and rear-mounting plate can be taken off.
With these parts removed, pull the pump away from the
cylinder block after removing the three securing bolts.

A more detailed description of the rotor-type oil pump
appears in Chapter II.

Fig. 31.—SHOWING RESULT OF
INCORRECTLY FITTING REAR-
CORK SEAL TO SUMP

If the seal is not seated
properly in its retaining
groove, the sump cannot be
pulled up tight and an oil
leak will occur.

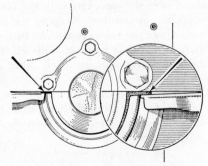

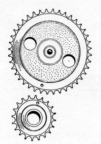

Fig. 32.—TO SET VALVE TIMING ON 'A' SERIES
ENGINE, THE TWO DOT MARKS ON THE SPROCKETS MUST
BE OPPOSITE ONE ANOTHER BEFORE THE CHAIN IS
FITTED

Valve Timing and Clearances

On the new Midget cars T.D.C. position for No. 1 and 4 cylinders can be found by turning the engine by its handle until the notch cut in the rear flange of the crankshaft pulley lines up with the longest of the pointers attached to the timing-chain cover. The two other pointers signify 10° and 5° before T.D.C.

The 1100 has a diamond-shaped cover on the top of the clutch housing and when this is removed the flywheel comes into view. T.D.C. position on this engine is when the $\frac{1}{4}$ marking on the flywheel rim comes into line with the pointer on the clutch housing visible through the inspection hole. Again both 10° and 5° before T.D.C. marks can be found on the flywheel.

Valve timing is by means of dot marks on the timing-chain sprockets and the Woodruff keys in the two shafts. Place the chain over the sprockets with the dot marks on each exactly opposite one another. Keeping the sprockets in this position note where the keyways are and turn the crankshaft and camshaft to the same position. Slide on the sprockets still keeping the dot marks opposite each other and the timing will be correct.

Setting of the valve-rocker gaps is carried out in the same way as for the Nuffield engine described earlier, the only difference being the gap, which should be 0·011 in. hot or 0·012 in. cold.

B.M.C. 'B' SERIES ENGINE

This basic engine has been used in various models over the years in a number of capacities: 1,489 c.c. in the MGA, Magnette ZA, ZB and Mark III; 1,588 c.c. in the MGA 1600 Mark I; 1,622 c.c. in the MGA 1600 Mark II and Magnette Mark IV; and at present it is using a new cylinder block that provides five main bearings and a capacity of 1,798 c.c. in the MGB and MGB GT models.

Sump Removal

Drain off the engine oil and undo the sump-securing bolts, removing them together with their washers. Should the sump not drop down past the front sub-frame crossmember, it means that the engine mountings and other connections have to be detached so that the engine can be raised on a pulley until the clutch housing is hard up against the underside of the bulkhead. In most cases this provides the necessary clearance to get the sump down, but if it does not then the engine will have to be lifted completely from the car. The oil strainer (when fitted) can be removed simply by undoing the two bolts that hold it to the sump cover.

Cylinder Head

The removal of this on all models is basically the same as the procedure outlined for the 'A' Series unit, for in fact the larger "B" Series engines are almost exactly the same, only scaled up.

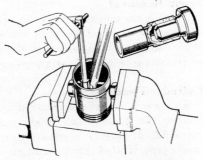

Fig. 33.—FITTING THE PISTONS TO THEIR CONNECTING RODS

Use plugs to hold the piston in a vice as shown in the inset. Do *not* clamp the vice directly on to the piston.

Oil Pump

The lubrication system differs from the 'A' Series engine only in the position and type of oil pump used. The larger engine has a gear-type pump, this being situated in the bottom of the crankcase and a strainer hangs below the pump in the sump to pick up the oil.

To remove the pump, the sump has to be taken off, the strainer removed, and the three nuts taken off the studs holding the pump body to the block. The pump can then be withdrawn together with its drive shaft (the pump being driven from a gear on the camshaft) and if it is being overhauled, the pump cover taken off.

Valve Timing and Clearances

Again, the method of timing the camshaft to the crankshaft is by means of sprockets and a roller chain. Timing is set by the dot marks on the sprockets and the Woodruff keys in the shafts as described under the 'A' Series unit, while the pointers and notch on the rear flange of the crankshaft pulley are provided for finding T.D.C. and the positions just before it.

All versions of this engine have the usual locknut and adjusting screw for setting the valve-rocker clearances, which are as follows (with engine cold). MGA, 0·018 in.; Magnette ZA, ZB, Mark III, MGA 1600 Mark I, 0·016 in.; MGA 1600 Mark II, Magnette Mark IV, MGB, MGB GT, 0·015 in.

MGA TWIN CAM ENGINE

Sump Removal

There is no difficulty with this operation, it merely being necessary to drain off the oil by removing the plug at the rear of the sump and then taking out the sump-securing bolts. The oil strainer is held to the pump cover by means of three bolts.

Cylinder Head

To remove the cylinder head, drain the cooling system and remove the header tank, thermostat housing and exhaust manifolds. It may be necessary to remove the heater water-intake pipe, if fitted. The exhaust manifolds can be removed by releasing the six nuts and washers holding the exhaust pipes to the manifolds, and then detaching the exhaust-pipe bracket from the gearbox mounting plate. The manifolds can then be parted from the cylinder head.

Remove the bolts and washers securing the cylinder-head water-intake pipe at the rear of the cylinder head. Disconnect the sparking-plug leads and remove the plugs. The camshaft covers should be removed and the camshafts disconnected from their driving chain; see under Timing Chain and Sprockets. Then remove the ten retaining nuts and lift off the cylinder-head.

When replacing the cylinder head always use a new gasket. Examine the seals fitted between the front camshaft bearings and the engine front plate and renew them if necessary. Tighten the cylinder-head nuts in the right sequence as shown in Fig. 34. The nuts should be tightened to 70 lb.–ft. torque and the remaining parts refitted opposite to their removal procedure.

Timing Chain and Sprockets

The arrangement of the timing chain can be seen in Fig. 36 (b). When the camshafts or cylinder head are to be removed it is first necessary to disconnect the camshaft driving sprockets from the driving flanges on the camshafts.

Take out the setscrews and washers securing the front end of each camshaft cover and the domed nuts along the top of each cover. Withdraw the covers and mark the camshaft sprockets and driving flanges so that they are refitted in the same positions.

Slacken the timing-chain adjuster as far as it will go. This is located beneath the oil-filler cap at the front end of the exhaust-camshaft cover. Remove the cap to gain access to the adjuster screw and locknut. When adjusting the chain tension, turn the adjusting screw in a clockwise direction until strong resistance is felt and then turn the screw back three-quarters of a turn; the chain will then have the correct amount of tension.

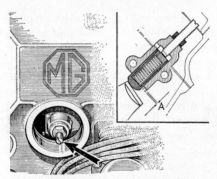

FIG. 35.—TIMING-CHAIN ADJUSTER ON THE MGA TWIN CAM

This is located below the oil-filler cap. A clearance of $\frac{1}{32}$ in. should be maintained at A to prevent the inner sleeve bottoming and the spring becoming inoperative.

Next remove the locking wire from the two setscrews securing each camshaft driving sprocket to the flange and slacken the screws. Slacken the two nuts holding the camshaft-sprocket support plate to the timing-chain cover. Pull the sprocket and support spindle away from the camshaft flange and engage the thread on the spindle with the support plate. Remove the sprocket setscrews completely.

When reassembling the sprockets to the camshafts, line up the marks made before removal and before fitting the sprocket securing screws. Do not forget to rewire the screws after they have been tightened.

Timing Chain Removal.—No attempt should be made to remove the timing chain unless special tools are available, as this operation also necessitates the removal of the timing-chain cover and the radiator. However, assuming that these parts have been removed, ensure that the **T** markings on the crankshaft and half-speed gears are lined up, i.e. adjacent to one another. Note that the distributor housing and driving gear are integral with the timing-chain cover.

Pistons and Connecting Rods

The piston and con-rod assemblies must be drawn up through the top of the bores to remove them. Once the sump has been lowered and the cylinder head removed, the big-end bearings should be disconnected. Be very careful not to score the cylinder walls. Keep the pistons and connecting rods in their correct order, and mark the bearing caps, connecting rods, etc. so they go back in the same cylinder and on the same journal.

The gudgeon pins are fully floating and can quite simply be released by removing their circlips. If wear is present on the small-end bearing, renew the bush; this should be a light press fit in the connecting rod. Ensure that the oil hole in the bush lines up with the oil hole in the connecting rod. Gudgeon pins should be a hand push fit into the small-end bush, do not attempt to ream or enlarge in any way.

Big-end bearings are of the shell type and require no hand finishing. As with the other engines, the shells are located by tabs in the bearing caps.

When fitting the pistons, see that the ring gaps are spaced at 180° to one another. Ensure that the big-end caps are facing the half-speed shaft side of the engine when they have been assembled.

Valve Clearances

The gap for both inlet and exhaust valves is 0·016–0·017 in. when the engine is cold. There is no valve adjustment as with push-rod operated valves, the correct clearance being maintained by the selection of shims which fit beneath the valve-stem head and the inverted barrel-type tappet. Shims are available in sixteen sizes from 0·086 in. (No. 1) to 0·116 in. (No. 16). Shims increase by 0·002 in. per number, e.g. No. 1 is 0·086 in, No. 2 is 0·088 in., No. 3 is 0·090 in. etc.

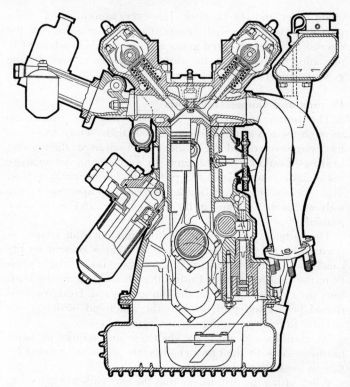

FIG. 36 (a).—CROSS-SECTION OF MGA TWIN CAM ENGINE

Turn the engine and check the clearance of each tappet; this should be measured at the back of the cam. To adjust the tappet clearances, disconnect the camshaft sprockets as described earlier and remove the camshafts. The tappets which require attention can be withdrawn by using a suction pad tool and the old shim removed. Insert a new shim of suitable thickness and when the camshaft has been refitted, check the clearance.

Variations in tappet clearance have a marked effect on the valve timing and it is suggested, therefore, that the valve timing is checked after adjusting the tappets.

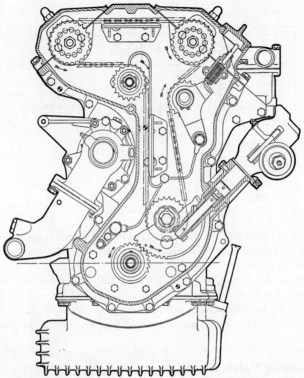

FIG. 36 (*b*).—THE TIMING CHAIN, TENSIONER AND DISTRIBUTOR DRIVE GEAR ON MGA TWIN CAM ENGINE

Checking Valve Timing

As explained earlier, variations in tappet clearance will affect the valve timing, so also will excessive chain stretch, and as a result the engine performance may suffer. Before checking the valve timing, therefore, first check the tappet clearances. To check the timing proceed as follows:

Mount a dial indicator to a suitable point on the cylinder head with the button resting on No. 1 inlet-valve tappet. Ensure that the cam is clear of the tappet and set the dial to zero. Turn the crankshaft until No. 1 piston is at T.D.C. with

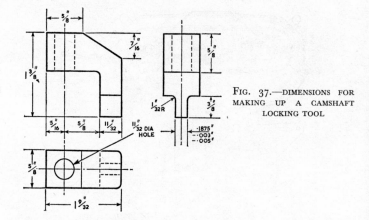

Fig. 37.—DIMENSIONS FOR MAKING UP A CAMSHAFT LOCKING TOOL

the valves rocking, i.e. No. 4 piston at T.D.C. on compression stroke, and line up the notch on the pulley with the pointer on the timing cover.

When the timing of the inlet camshaft is correct, the dial indicator will show that the tappet has moved between 0·069 and 0·082 in. Exactly the same reading should be obtained for the exhaust camshaft, which should be checked in the same way.

Adjusting Valve Timing

If the timing is incorrect it can be altered by removing the timing cover and knocking back the lockwasher on the chain-adjuster securing bolts, withdrawing the adjuster. Swing the adjuster sprocket fork clear of the timing chain and rotate the camshafts until the slots in the inner flanges line up with the slots in the front-camshaft bearing housings. The camshaft should now be locked into position and this can best be done by using a special tool which can be made up according to Fig. 37. First see that the **T** markings are in correct register and that No. 1 piston is at T.D.C.

Remove the camshaft-sprocket locating screws and slacken the sprocket-support spindles. Turn the inlet-camshaft sprocket in a clockwise direction to pull the chain tight between the half-speed gear and the inlet-camshaft sprocket. If two opposite holes in the sprocket do not line-up exactly with the tappet holes in the camshaft flange, it will be necessary to use the vernier arrangement provided by the holes in the camshaft sprocket. The differential between one hole spacing and two wheel teeth is 1·2° of camshaft rotation.

Lift the chain off the camshaft sprocket and turn the sprocket to select a pair of holes which will line-up exactly with the tapped holes in the camshaft flange when the chain is tight. When the correct holes have been located, fit the sprocket-securing screws and tighten the support spindle. Detach the locking tool from the inlet camshaft and carry out the same operation for the exhaust camshaft, ensuring that the chain tension between the exhaust, inlet and half-speed sprockets is maintained. Once all the components have been reassembled, adjust the tension of the chain as detailed earlier and once again check the valve timing with the aid of the dial indicator. If the timing is correct, rewire the sprocket-securing screws and fit the camshaft covers.

COOLING SYSTEM

The usual type cooling system is employed on all cars, using a water pump and thermostat. There are two drain points, one being on the cylinder block and the other in the bottom of the radiator. Note that the heater unit cannot be drained. To give safe protection during winter, use an anti-freeze solution.

The system can be filled by closing the drain points and pouring the fresh water in through the radiator filler, except in the case of the 1100 model which has a partially-sealed system with overflow tank. With this model, the following special procedure has to be carried out when filling the system. Fill the radiator to the top of the filler neck, replace the radiator cap, run the engine until hot and then allow it to cool. The radiator is filled again and the same operation carried out three times until the overflow tank has sufficient water in it. With this model *never* remove the radiator cap with the engine hot, it is dangerous with normal cars, but on this system severe scalding can result.

CHAPTER VI

CLUTCH

THE clutches used on models covered by this book can be divided into two distinct types, the conventional Borg & Beck single dry plate and the B.M.C. single dry plate designed specifically for the front-wheel drive (f.w.d.) 1100 car with its transverse engine and underslung transmission.

ADJUSTMENT FOR CLUTCH WEAR

Both types of clutch will be described fully later in the chapter, but first methods of adjustment to take up wear can be covered, although it will only apply to certain models.

On cars having hydraulically-actuated clutches there is no mechanical adjustment (except the f.w.d. 1100), wear on the clutch parts being taken care of automatically by the master and slave cylinders. When the time comes that clutch slip or difficulty in engaging gear appears, it means that the clutch has to be overhauled.

On other models, mechanical adjustment for the clutch to compensate for wear is generally under the car and situated on the connecting rod between the pedal and the operating lever that passes through the clutch housing. There should always be about $\frac{3}{4}$ in. free play on the clutch pedal to ensure that the full pressure of the clutch springs is bearing down on the centre plate, thus making sure no slip is occurring.

To make the adjustment, the locknut on the pedal rod must be slackened and the second nut turned until the correct free play at the pedal is reached, then the locknut tightened again. If the clutch-pedal return spring has to be removed to make the adjustment, always make sure it is replaced properly, otherwise the clutch runs all the time as if the driver's foot is resting upon the pedal.

Fig. 38.—ADJUSTING CLUTCH CLEARANCE ON THE FRONT-WHEEL DRIVE 1100

The front-wheel drive 1100 has a different method of adjustment for pedal free play, the pedal itself not being used as the measuring device. Adjustment is carried out under the bonnet, where the long clutch-operating lever can be seen connecting the slave cylinder to the withdrawal boss in the centre of the clutch housing. About half-way along the length of the operating lever is an abutment which comes up against a bolt and locknut; to set the clutch clearance the lever must be pulled away from the slave cylinder until its free travel is taken up, and then the gap between the abutment and bolt head should measure 0·020 in. If it does not, the locknut must be slackened and the bolt turned until the gap is correct.

CLUTCH OVERHAUL

As either the engine or gearbox has to be removed to gain access to the clutch it is common practice to overhaul the clutch at the same time as the engine. However, a clutch may wear out before either of the other units requires attention and

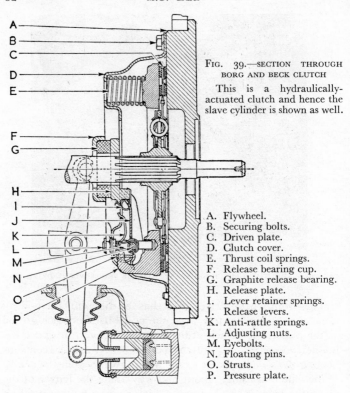

FIG. 39.—SECTION THROUGH BORG AND BECK CLUTCH

This is a hydraulically-actuated clutch and hence the slave cylinder is shown as well.

A. Flywheel.
B. Securing bolts.
C. Driven plate.
D. Clutch cover.
E. Thrust coil springs.
F. Release bearing cup.
G. Graphite release bearing.
H. Release plate.
I. Lever retainer springs.
J. Release levers.
K. Anti-rattle springs.
L. Adjusting nuts.
M. Eyebolts.
N. Floating pins.
O. Struts.
P. Pressure plate.

then the following procedure has to be adopted on all models except the front-wheel drive 1100.

Remove the gearbox from the car as described in the next chapter and undo the bolts around the circumference of the clutch assembly, a little at a time, to avoid distortion. When they are all removed, the clutch can be withdrawn from the flywheel, noting that it is located there by dowels and marking it so that replacement is affected with it in the same position. Both the pressure-plate assembly and the centre plate will come free.

A carbon-release pad is held in the operating fork by means of two spring clips pushed in from each side; these can be released with a screwdriver and the pad taken out of the fork. All the parts can then be examined for wear; if the centre-plate linings are worn down, have traces of oil, or are loose, then a replacement plate is required. If the carbon portion of the release pad is worn this, too, must be renewed. The pressure-plate assembly relies on the correct setting of its three release levers and the correct strength of its springs (or plate spring in the diaphragm spring unit) for proper functioning and special equipment is needed to test and set these.

Naturally, any signs of wear, burning or cracking of the pressure-plate surface means that the complete assembly must be changed, but if the plate appears satisfactory and there is no sign of wear on the release levers, the springs are all tight and nothing can be seen to be broken, then quite often a clutch

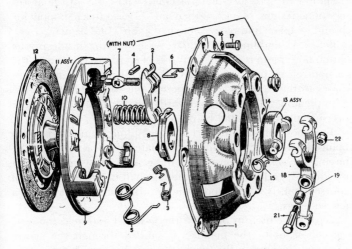

FIG. 40.—EXPLODED VIEW OF BORG AND BECK CLUTCH

1. Clutch cover.	10. Pressure-plate spring.	16. Cover-screw spring washers.
2. Release lever.	11. Driven-plate assembly.	17. Cover to flywheel screw.
3. Lever retainer.	12. Lining.	18. Withdrawal-lever assembly.
4. Lever pin.	13. Thrust-ring assembly.	19. Bush.
5. Anti-rattle spring.	14. Carbon ring.	21. Lever bolt.
6. Strut.	15. Retainer.	22. Bolt nut.
7. Eyebolt with nut.		
8. Bearing thrust plate.		
9. Pressure plate.		

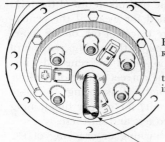

FIG. 41.—CENTRING THE CLUTCH DURING REFITMENT USING A MANDREL OR GUIDE

The mandrel (arrowed) is being used to line up the centre plate before tightening the securing bolts.

overhaul need only mean the replacement of the centre plate and carbon pad.

Should the pressure-plate assembly show any of the afore-mentioned signs of wear, then all three clutch components should be taken and part exchanged at an M.G. dealer.

Before assembling the clutch, wash out the inside of the clutch housing to remove any traces of oil or grease, and fit the carbon-release pad to the fork. Offer up the pressure and centre plates to the flywheel, remembering the centre plate is fitted with the long side of its hub towards the rear of the car and the pressure plate is located by dowels.

The most important part of assembling comes next, this being the alignment of the centre plate. A mandrel, or guide, having the same dimensions as the gearbox first-motion shaft is required, and if an old first-motion shaft is available this is of course ideal. If not, a guide can be turned up on a lathe for a few shillings.

With the clutch in place on the flywheel and held there by very loose bolts, the mandrel is pushed through the centre plate and located in the flywheel spigot bearing. Keeping the mandrel in this position, the securing bolts can be tightened evenly, a little at a time, so the clutch is pulled down without distortion. When tight, the mandrel is removed as the centre plate will be gripped tight between the flywheel and the pressure plate.

Upon replacing the gearbox, its first-motion shaft will now fit easily into the clutch, whereas if no centre-plate aligning

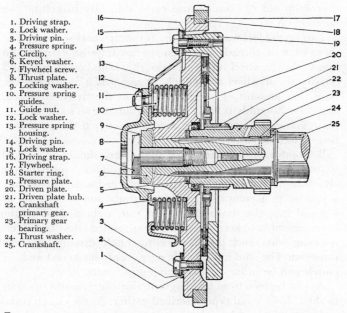

1. Driving strap.
2. Lock washer.
3. Driving pin.
4. Pressure spring.
5. Circlip.
6. Keyed washer.
7. Flywheel screw.
8. Thrust plate.
9. Locking washer.
10. Pressure spring guides.
11. Guide nut.
12. Lock washer.
13. Pressure spring housing.
14. Driving pin.
15. Lock washer.
16. Driving strap.
17. Flywheel.
18. Starter ring.
19. Pressure plate.
20. Driven plate.
21. Driven plate hub.
22. Crankshaft primary gear.
23. Primary gear bearing.
24. Thrust washer.
25. Crankshaft.

FIG. 42.—SECTION THROUGH CLUTCH USED ON FRONT-WHEEL DRIVE 1100

was carried out, no matter how much pushing took place, if the plate was not central the gearbox would not fit, instead it would probably push the middle hub out of the centre plate.

Front-wheel Drive 1100 Clutch

As there is no gearbox to take out of this transverse-engined car, the complete power unit has to have all its mountings and other connections disconnected so that it can be lifted just enough to take off the clutch cover, after removing the necessary bolts around its circumference.

The three nuts securing the thrust pad to the clutch cover can be undone and the engine then turned to the T.D.C. position for No. 1 cylinder so that the complete flywheel and clutch assembly can be removed. If the engine is not turned to this position first, the 'C' washer locating the primary gear may drop out of position and cause difficulty in getting the flywheel off.

Tap up the lockwasher and undo the flywheel-securing bolt three or four threads and then use an impulse extractor to break the flywheel taper. Undo the bolt completely and remove the flywheel and clutch, *keeping it in a vertical position*. A certain amount of oil will remain in the flywheel oil-seal and if the assembly is tilted this could run out on to the centre-plate linings. Of course, this does not matter if the plate is to be renewed anyway.

Before dismantling the clutch all the parts should be marked so that they are assembled in the same positions, especially the clutch-to-flywheel driving straps. To proceed with dismantling, a special tool comprising of three studs and nuts must be screwed into the flywheel and the nuts tightened on to the cover assembly to keep the springs compressed while the cover-securing nuts and the flywheel-to-clutch driving pins are removed. The stud nuts can then be evenly slackened and the clutch will be in its separate component parts.

As can be seen from the diagram, this clutch works opposite to the conventional type described earlier. As the clutch pedal is depressed, the release bearing is forced down on to a thrust pad, pushing the clutch cover on to the pressure springs, and due to the driving pins, moving the pressure plate away from the centre plate, thus allowing the centre plate to revolve freely and thereby transmitting no drive to the primary gear.

With the clutch dismantled, examine the parts for wear—again, any signs of wear on the centre plate, or oil, burn marks, or cracks on either of the plates renders them useless. Having obtained the new parts (none of which are available on the part-exchange scheme), reassemble the clutch, using the special tool to compress the pressure springs and then refit the complete unit to the power pack.

Diaphragm-spring Clutch

On the MGB and the MGB GT models, the clutch-cover assembly is fitted with a diaphragm-type plate spring instead of the series of coil springs. All of the preceding instruction for

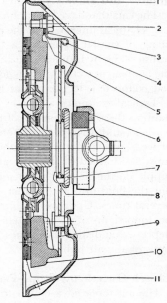

FIG. 43.—SECTION THROUGH
DIAPHRAGM-SPRING CLUTCH FITTED TO
MGB MODELS

1. Cover.
2. Strap bolt.
3. Washer.
4. Clip.
5. Strap.
6. Release bearing.
7. Release plate.
8. Circlip—release plate.
9. Diaphragm spring.
10. Pressure plate.
11. Driven plate.

gaining access and removing the clutch components is the same for these models, the only differences come when dismantling the pressure-plate assembly. This must be carried out as follows:

Remove the circlip securing the thrust pad to the diaphragm and lift off the pad. Unscrew the three screws securing the clips to the pressure plate, a turn at a time, until the diaphragm comes into contact with the cover. Then take out the screws, clips and washers and the pressure plate. Turn the release-bearing spring-retaining clips through 90° and withdraw the bearing from its fork, if this too is to be changed.

The advantage of the diaphragm-spring clutch is that it takes up less space, being much narrower in section than the older coil-spring assemblies, and also the diaphragm spring, because of its shorter travel, gives a more progressive take up of the clutch with much less chance of judder.

Master and Slave Cylinders

The cars that have hydraulic actuation of the clutch all have a mechanical linkage from the pedal to a master cylinder, this being of similar design to a brake master cylinder. Piping transfers the hydraulic pressure to a slave cylinder (this being the equivalent to the brake wheel cylinder), which has a push-rod connection to the actual lever that operates the clutch.

Typical examples are shown in the diagrams, and over-hauling these units consists of renewing the rubber seals and washers, and perhaps the pistons as well if they show any signs of wear. When disturbing either of the cylinders, the system must be drained of fluid by attaching a rubber tube to the nipple on the slave cylinder, opening it a turn and pumping out the fluid into a container by operating the clutch pedal several times. Upon assembling the master cylinder, it has to be topped up and the system bled until the pedal can be depressed and the fluid comes from the bleed nipple with no signs of any air bubbles.

Clutch Overthrow Stop—Front-wheel Drive 1100

Having replaced a clutch to the 1100, the overthrow stop should be reset. As well as the gap at the operating lever, the

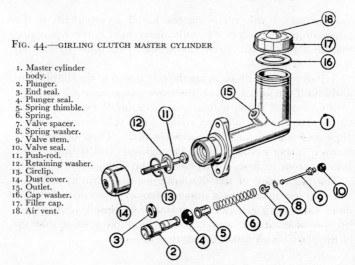

FIG. 44.—GIRLING CLUTCH MASTER CYLINDER

1. Master cylinder body.
2. Plunger.
3. End seal.
4. Plunger seal.
5. Spring thimble.
6. Spring.
7. Valve spacer.
8. Spring washer.
9. Valve stem.
10. Valve seal.
11. Push-rod.
12. Retaining washer.
13. Circlip.
14. Dust cover.
15. Outlet.
16. Cap washer.
17. Filler cap.
18. Air vent.

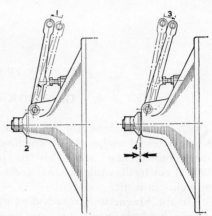

FIG. 45.—ADJUSTING CLUTCH
OVERTHROW STOP ON
FRONT-WHEEL DRIVE 1100

1 and 2 shows the clutch
fully released with the overthrow stop screwed up to
the casing. 3 and 4 is the
clutch fully engaged and
the stop screwed up a
further 0·007–0·010 in. as
described in the text.

overthrow stop on the boss must be properly set to make sure
there is no advance wear on the components. To do this, screw
the stop and locknut away from the clutch cover to the limit of
its travel, then depress the clutch pedal to fully release the
clutch and hold it in this position. Screw up the stop to the
cover, release the clutch pedal and then screw up the stop
another 0·007–0·010 in. (about 1 flat on the hexagon) before
fully tightening the locknut.

Recheck the gap at the operating-lever adjuster as described
earlier and adjust again if necessary.

CHAPTER VII

GEARBOX

SINCE the end of the war, all gearboxes fitted to M.G. cars have been four-speed with synchromesh on the upper three ratios only. These gears that are in constant mesh have helical cut teeth, while the first and reverse gear wheels have straight-cut teeth.

On the Magnette Farina-bodied models, automatic transmission has been an optional extra since the introduction of the 1,622 c.c. engine, while the MGB models have overdrive as optional equipment.

Gearbox Removal

This job is tackled differently depending upon whether or not the model concerned has removable floor panels in the front. If it has, then generally the gearbox is removed via the inside of the car, but with no floor panels the gearbox is taken out from under the vehicle. Of course, the gear-change lever has to be taken out before commencing the removing.

The propeller shaft must be disconnected as well as the linkage to the clutch-operating arm that passes through the bell housing; undo the speedometer drive cable and take out the bell-housing bolts. The engine must then be supported while the gearbox mountings are removed, together with the sub-frame cross-shaft if this is of the removable type; in some cases the engine has rear mountings that must be disconnected.

Should the top bell-housing bolts be inaccessible, the engine has to have its front mountings disconnected and the engine lowered so that the unit tilts to bring the bolts into view. With all the necessary parts disconnected, the gearbox can be drawn rearwards off the clutch, turned slightly to one side, and withdrawn from under the car—or withdrawn into the car through the gap left by the removable floor panels.

With the M.G. 1100, the complete power pack has to be taken out employing one of the methods described in Chapter V. Then the nuts around the bottom of the crankcase are removed so that the engine can be lifted off the transmission case, leaving the gearbox internal parts exposed.

Dismantling Gearbox

All the detachable parts of the gearbox casing, such as the gear-lever tower or extension, the rear extension, the side cover or, in some cases, the bell housing, should be taken off and the clutch fork and cross-shaft removed. When the selector forks are exposed their square-headed screws locating them on the shafts can be taken out, the shafts drifted clear, and the forks lifted out.

Different gearboxes now have different procedures, although most require the layshaft to be drifted out so that its gear cluster can drop to the bottom of the box. Generally, early models (pre-B.M.C.) have their first-motion shaft removed by drifting its bearing toward the front, then the mainshaft can be drifted to the rear far enough to displace its rear bearing—which is removed together with its guard—allowing the mainshaft to be withdrawn out of the top of the box.

With B.M.C. gearboxes, the mainshaft must be tapped forward to displace the first-motion shaft, then tapped to the rear to knock out the rear bearing, which then gives room for the mainshaft to be extracted from the top of the casing.

If there is a detachable plate inside the clutch housing, this has to be removed with its oil seal and shims, before the layshaft can be drifted out. There is also a large nut holding the first-motion shaft in place. The mainshaft has to be drifted out to the rear, the reverse gear and shaft taken out, and then the first-motion shaft drifted out to the front.

Work on the 1100 gearbox proceeds through the wide opening of the transmission case top, after first taking off the differential housing and change-speed-lever extension. The selector forks and rods are removed in the usual way and the mainshaft-bearing retainer taken off the centre web of the casing. The layshaft can be drifted out of the case and the gear cluster lifted clear, then the first-motion shaft can have its

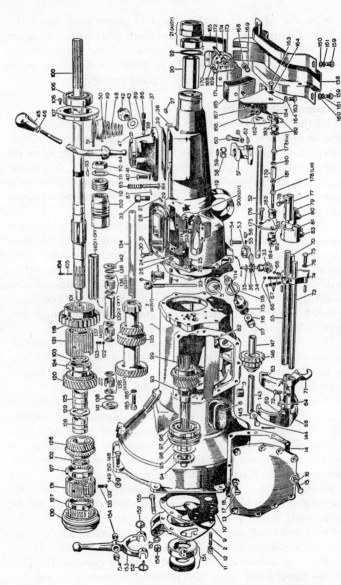

FIG. 46.—EXPLODED VIEW OF MAGNETTE ZA AND ZB GEARBOX. For key to numbers, see facing page.

KEY TO FIG. 46

1. Gearbox casing.
2. Front cover stud.
3. Drain plug.
4. Gearbox extension stud.
5. Blanking plug.
6. Dust cover with insert.
7. Dipstick.
8. Felt.
9-12. Front cover, joint, stud nut and spring washer.
13-18. Side cover, joint, set-screw, spring washer, countersunk screw and shake-proof washer.
19. Gearbox extension.
20. Extension bush.
21. Oil-seal assembly.
22. Oil-seal joint.
23-26. Extension to gearbox joint, stud nut, set-screw and spring washer.
27. Taper plug.
28-31. Extension side cover, joint, set-screw and spring washer.
32. Breather assembly.
33-36. Oil-level valve-assembly body, circlip, plate and valve-body joint.
37-41. Change-speed lever tower, dowel, joint, set-screw and spring washer.
42. Reverse-light switch.
43. Switch joint.
44-51. Change-speed lever, knob, lock-nut, lever-ball snug, spring, retaining washer, spring cover and circlip.
52. Remote-control shaft.

53-56. Front selector lever, set-screw, spring washer and lever key.
57-62. Rear selector lever, bush, circlip, set-screw, spring washer and key.
63-67. 1st- and 2nd-speed fork, locating screw, shaft, ball and spring.
68-70. 3rd- and 4th-speed fork, locating screw and shaft.
71-73. Reverse fork, locating screw and shaft.
74. Shafts locating block.
75. Block to casing set-screw.
76. Screw spring washer.
77, 78. 1st- and 2nd-gear selector and screw.
79, 80. 3rd- and 4th-gear selector and screw.
81. Reverse-gear selector.
82. Change-speed gate.
83. Selector locating screw.
84-89. Reverse-selector plunger, spring, plug, dowel, ball and spring.
90. Interlock with plate arm.
91. Plate to casing :set-screw.
92. Spring washer.
93-99. 1st-motion shaft, nut, lock-washer, ball bearing, spring ring, shim and needle rollers.
100. 3rd-motion shaft.
101. Oil restrictor.
102. Front thrust washer.
103. Rear thrust washer.
104. Front thrust-washer prg.
105. Peg spring.
106. 3rd-motion-shaft rear bearing.

107. Bearing housing.
108. Locating peg.
109-113. Speedometer gear distance-piece, nut, lock-washer, gear and key.
114-118. Speedometer-drive pinion, bush, oil seal, retaining ring and joint.
119. 1st-speed gear.
120. 2nd-speed gear.
121. 2nd-speed synchroniser.
122. Synchroniser ball.
123. Ball spring.
124. 2nd-speed gear baulk ring.
125. 2nd-speed gear bush.
126. 3rd-speed gear.
127. 3rd- and 4th- gear baulk ring.
128. 3rd-speed gear bush.
129. 2nd- and 3rd-gear bushes interlocking ring.
130, 131. 3rd- and 4th-speed sliding coupling and gear synchroniser.
132. Synchroniser ball.
133. Ball spring.
134-138. Layshaft, gear, outer needle-roller bearing, inner needle-roller bearing and spring ring.
139, 140. Bearing distance-piece.
141. Front thrust washer.
142. Rear thrust washer.
143. Reverse shaft.
144. Shaft locking-screw.
145. Screw lock-washer.
146, 147. Reverse gear and bush.
148-150. Gearbox-to-mounting plate bolt, nut and spring washer.
151. Release assembly bearing.

152. Bearing retainer.
153, 154. Clutch-withdrawal lever and bush.
155-157. Lever to front cover bolt, nut and washer.
158-161. Rear mounting assembly with right-hand bracket cross-member, body screw, plain washer and spring washer.
162-164. Left-hand cross-member bracket, screw and washer.
165-167. Rear rubber mounting, nut and spring washer.
168. Mounting rubber to gearbox bracket nut.
169. Spring washer.
170. Right-hand gearbox mounting bracket.
171. Left-hand gearbox mounting bracket.
172-174. Rear mounting spigot stud, nut and spring washer.
175. Engine-steady bracket.
176. Steady bracket to gearbox extension bolt.
177. Right-hand thread engine-control link.
178. Left-hand thread engine control link.
179. Adjuster nut.
180. Right-hand thread link lock-nut.
181. Left-hand thread link lock-nut.
182, 183. Link cup and rubber.
184. Cross-member and gearbox lock-nut.
185, 186. Starter to engine screw and washer.

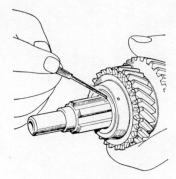

Fig. 47.—DISMANTLING MAINSHAFT

The 3rd-speed gear collar-locating plunger must be depressed so that the gear can be slid from the shaft.

circlip and roller bearings removed, its nut taken off, and the shaft and gear removed.

The mainshaft can be taken out by drifting it to the rear far enough to get a spacer interposed between first-speed gear and the bearing, then drifting it forward again until the bearing is out of its housing. Once the bearing is off the shaft it can be removed from the casing.

Stripping Mainshaft

The assembly of the gears and synchromesh cones on the mainshaft is very similar in all models and the Midget unit (from 1961) can be used as an example. Withdraw the top-

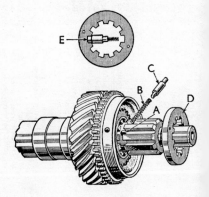

Fig. 48.—SECURING PLUNGERS FOR MAINSHAFT GEARS ON MAGNETTE SERIES III AND IV GEARBOX

A. Spring hole.
B. Spring.
C. Locating peg.
D. Lock washer.
E. Peg located in washer.

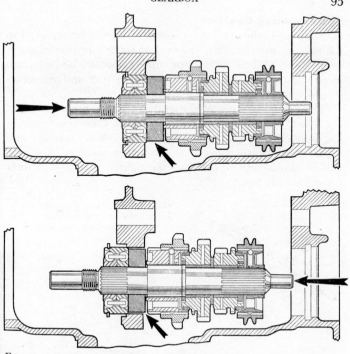

FIG. 49.—METHOD OF REMOVING MAINSHAFT BEARING ON FRONT-WHEEL DRIVE
1100 USING SPECIAL TOOL

The shaft is drifted to the back and the spacer inserted, it can then be
drifted in the other direction and the bearing is forced out

and third-speed synchromesh hub from the forward end of the
shaft and remove the front thrust washer by pressing down the
spring-loaded locating plunger and turning the washer until
the splines line up. Then remove the gear, plunger and spring,
followed by the third-gear bush and interlocking ring. Withdraw the second-speed gear and bush and take off the rear
thrust washer and first-speed gear and hub.

If the synchromesh assemblies are dismantled further, wrap
the unit in a piece of rag before pushing the sliding dog from
the synchro unit. This will make sure the three springs and
balls that are located in the hub do not fly out and get lost.

Reassembling Gearbox

In all cases, the gearbox components should be replaced in the reverse order to their removal, making sure everything is quite clean. When assembling the mainshaft, all the hub assemblies should slide freely on their splines and the gears should rotate with no undue friction.

For proper meshing of the gear teeth, the drive gear and mainshaft bearings must be fitted tight in their housings and the layshaft must be assembled with new thrust washers and needle-roller bearings to obtain the correct end-float. Use new gaskets throughout and if possible tighten the nuts to their correct torque figures.

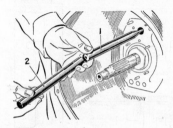

FIG. 50 (*left*).—WHEN FITTING A LAY-SHAFT (2) USE A PILOT SHAFT (1) TO ENSURE NO NEEDLE BEARINGS ARE DISPLACED

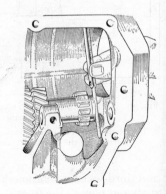

FIG. 51 (*right*).—CHECKING LAYSHAFT CLUSTER-GEAR END-FLOAT ON MAG-NETTE SERIES III AND IV

The end-float should be 0·002–0·003 in.

Gearbox Faults

Most gearboxes give good service until their bearings wear, the gear-teeth chip, and a noise is set up. This will probably, in time, result in a completely broken gear, which will entail a full overhaul or a manufacturer's reconditioned unit. There are two other faults which sometimes come to light at shorter intervals and if put right then will give the unit another lease of life, these being: (1) difficult or noisy gear engagement, and (2) automatic disengagement of the gears.

Difficult or Noisy Engagement

The first check that must always be made when a car suffers from noise during gear engagement is with the clutch, for if the pedal adjustment is wrong, or the clutch is worn, then the drive from the engine is not being cut off completely and the gear teeth will grate as they move into mesh. In the case of hydraulic-actuated clutches, the system may require bleeding or be short of fluid.

Difficult engagement could be due to tightness on the selector forks and shafts, or wear on their detents; perhaps with the remote-control change mechanism of M.G. cars there is wear present on the rods and couplings between the change-speed lever and the actual selector gate in the box. Another cause for difficult and noisy engagement is wear on the synchromesh hubs and cones so they are not synchronising the gears before the selectors are moving the sliding dog over. If a gearbox is to be dismantled to fit new synchromesh assemblies, it may just as well be completely overhauled.

Automatic Disengagement

In the main this complaint, of a gear jumping out when under load, is caused by one or more of the following:

(a) Wear on the selector rod adjacent to the recess for the detent plunger.

(b) A weak detent spring or worn plunger.

(c) A loose locking screw on the selector fork.

(d) Wear on the synchromesh sliding dog and its inter-locking balls and spring.

All of these necessitate the removal of the gearbox and partial dismantling to ascertain the fault and rectify it.

BORG-WARNER AUTOMATIC TRANSMISSION

The Farina-styled Magnette models may be fitted with an automatic gearbox that is driven via a torque converter, there being no separate clutch operation and no gear lever as such. A selector quadrant is mounted on the steering column, this having positions for Drive, Park, Neutral, Low and Reverse. It is a three-speed transmission which can be over-ridden and

D

held in either of the two lower ratios by movement of the selector lever at the necessary times. The only maintenance required by this transmission is periodic checks on the fluid level.

Repair of the automatic transmission is beyond the capabilities of the average owner since special tools are required and the home garage is invariably too dusty for assembly of the mechanism in any case. This matter of cleanliness must always be borne in mind if long and trouble-free transmission life is to be expected; make sure that any fluid added is brand new and wipe the area around the filler perfectly clean.

Only the recommended grades of automatic-transmission fluid must be put in the box and it is not desirable to mix name brands, so if a car with automatic drive is bought, find out the make of fluid in the unit. The recommended brands and grades are as follows:

Duckhams Nolmatic; Shell Donax T6; BP Energol ATF Type A; Mobilfluid 200; Castrol TQ; Filtrate Super AG; Sternol Lynx; Esso Automatic Fluid Grade 55.

To check fluid level, the car must be standing on a level surface with the selector lever in 'L', the handbrake on, and the engine idling at normal running temperature. Access to the dipstick is gained by lifting the bonnet; take a reading on this by removing it, wiping it clean, replacing and withdrawing it almost immediately; add fluid to bring the reading to the 'High' mark if necessary.

The difference between the 'High' and 'Low' marks is one pint, so be very careful to not overfill the transmission.

CHAPTER VIII

BRAKES, WHEELS AND TYRES

ALL models except Twin Cam and Farina-styled Magnettes have Lockheed hydraulic systems using either drums on all four wheels, or disc/drum combinations. The Twin Cam is fitted with Dunlop disc brakes all round, while the Farina-styled Magnettes (from Mark III) have Girling drum brakes. The actual hydraulic system is of a similar layout regardless of the type of brakes used; the foot pedal is coupled to a master cylinder that is fed with fluid from its reservoir and this generates the pressure along the pipelines to the brake shoe or pad actuating cylinders and pistons at each wheel.

Master Cylinder

This unit is probably the most important single item in the braking system as it is linked directly to all four wheels and any fault in the cylinder will affect all the four brakes. The master cylinder is connected via a push rod to the foot pedal, while the actual cylinder part has two drillings through to the fluid reservoir and contains a piston, piston-rubber cup, return spring, dished washer and the push rod which bears on to the piston and moves it down the cylinder in relation to foot-pedal travel.

As the pedal is depressed, the piston moves and its cup immediately shuts off the drilling that connects the bore to the reservoir. The fluid present is forced out past a valve in the end of the cylinder and the resulting pressure along the pipes moves the four wheel-cylinder pistons out and brings the shoes into contact with the drums, or the pads into contact with the discs.

When the brake pedal is released, the return spring takes over and pushes the piston back along its bore, while the brake-shoe return springs squeeze the wheel cylinder pistons

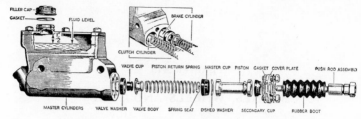

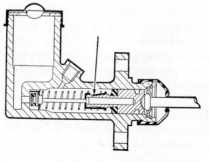

FIG. 52.—EXPLODED VIEW OF TANDEM BRAKE AND CLUTCH MASTER CYLINDER
FITTED TO MAGNETTE ZA, ZB, AND MGA

back also. The resultant back-pressure lifts the master-
cylinder outlet valve off its seat, so long as the pressure is
stronger than the master-cylinder spring.

Cars that have a hydraulic clutch usually have a separate
master cylinder on the same lines as the above connected to
the clutch-operating slave cylinder—the two master cylinders
can be found mounted side-by-side under the bonnet.

Master Cylinder Overhaul

This can only be carried out with the master cylinder
removed from the car, a job that generally only entails the
disconnecting of the feed pipes and pedal yoke and the
removal of the mounting bolts. The first step of overhauling is
the taking off of the rubber dust excluder and end cover, or
circlip, when all the internal parts can be withdrawn, their
order of fitment being carefully noted.

FIG. 53.—SECTION THROUGH
GIRLING MASTER CYLINDER

The arrow indicates the
thimble leaf valve.

Obviously all the rubbers have to be renewed during overhaul, as should the piston if it shows signs of scoring; if this also
applies to the walls of the cylinder you are best advised to buy a
factory-reconditioned unit. Soak all the rubbers in brake fluid
and as the piston is pushed into its bore make quite sure the lip
of the rubber cup does not turn back. All parts must be perfectly clean during assembly. After securing the master
cylinder in place, those having an adjustable push-rod should
be set to give $\frac{1}{2}$ in. free play at the pedal before the piston
starts to move along the cylinder.

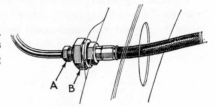

Fig. 54.—TO REMOVE A FLEX-
IBLE BRAKE HOSE ALWAYS
DISCONNECT PIPE NUT 'A' FIRST,
THEN UNSCREW LOCKNUT 'B.'

Maintaining Fluid Level

The fluid level in the master-cylinder reservoir should be
kept about $\frac{1}{2}$ in. below the filler neck and this level should be
checked at the periods listed in Chapter I. Use only Lockheed
Brake Fluid on all drum-braked models except Magnette III
and IV—these use Girling Crimson fluid. Disc-braked cars use
Dunlop recommended fluid for the Twin Cam, and Lockheed
Series 2 Disc Brake Fluid for the others.

Pipe Lines

The fluid supply to the wheel cylinders is carried through
copper or steel pipes which are clipped to the vehicle frame.
To permit movement of the wheels, short flexible pipes carry
the fluid the last few inches to the rear of the brake. No maintenance of the metal pipes is required, although they should
be examined occasionally for signs of looseness or chafing.

After considerable service, or earlier if incorrect fluid is used,
the flexible hoses may suffer from internal swelling or slight
seepage from their metal ends and the only rectification for
this is to renew the hose concerned.

To do this, always start at the end of the hose nearest the master cylinder. The union on the steel pipe is undone first, followed by the large nut retaining the hose to its bracket or the body frame; while doing this a second spanner is required to stop the hose from twisting up. Lastly the other end of the hose can be unscrewed from the brake back-plate (or disc-caliper assembly). The new hose can be fitted in the reverse order to this.

Wheel Cylinders, Shoes and Drums

There are generally two front-wheel cylinders and only one rear, the former being firmly affixed to the back-plate, and the latter having some up-and-down movement so that the shoes centralise themselves inside the drum during operation of the handbrake.

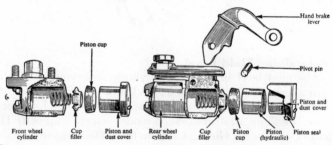

FIG. 55.—FRONT- AND REAR-WHEEL CYLINDER COMPONENTS OF MGA MODELS

Inside the wheel cylinder is a single piston and a rubber cup, the trailing edge of the brake shoe resting on the flat end of the piston. As fluid pressure is felt behind the rubber cup and piston they are pushed along the cylinder, bringing the brake shoes into contact with the drum. A bleed screw, to remove air from the system, can be found on each back-plate located in one of the wheel cylinders.

The wheel cylinders can have their internal parts dismantled while they are still attached to the back-plate, thus making cleaning and fitting of new rubbers quite easy, but any score marks or other signs of wear in the bore itself means the cylinder must be renewed. The order of fitment of the wheel

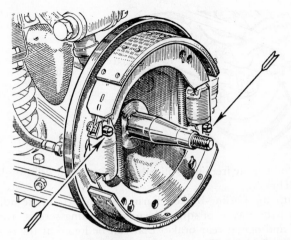

FIG. 56.—FRONT-BRAKE DRUM REMOVED TO SHOW THE "MICRAM" ADJUSTERS
USED ON LOCKHEED BRAKES

cylinder parts are: rubber dust excluder, piston, rubber cup
and spring.

On some models, the short handbrake lever that passes
through each back-plate is part of the wheel cylinder, being
held in place by a pivot pin and levering the piston out
mechanically when the handbrake is pulled on. In other cases,
the lever works directly on to the shoes via a link arm.

Brake Adjustment—Drum Brakes

On all models except the Farina Magnettes, Twin Cam,
1100, MGA 1600 Mark II, MGB 1800 and front brakes of
MGA 1600 Mark I, the method of adjusting the brakes to take
up clearance between the shoe linings and the drums is the
same. There are holes drilled through the front face of the
brake drum which will take a screwdriver; the brake drum
has to be rotated until the 'Micram' adjusting screw(s)
become visible (there are two on each front brake and only one
on each rear) and then the screwdriver inserted and the
adjuster turned until the drum is locked. Then turn back
adjuster until it is heard to 'click' once, when the brake drum

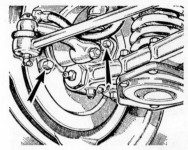

FIG. 57.—BRAKE ADJUSTERS ON
GIRLING SYSTEM FITTED TO MAG-
NETTE SERIES III AND IV
Similar adjusters are used on
the rear brakes of the 1100.

should be quite free; if it still rubs stiffly turn the adjuster back
two 'clicks'.

With the Girling-braked Farina Magnettes, brake adjustment is by means of square-headed adjusting screws (two at
front and one at rear brake) that can be found at the rear of
each back-plate. These can be screwed in until the brake is
locked, and then turned slowly back until the drum revolves
freely. This is also the method of adjusting the rear brakes of
1100, MGA 1600 Mark II and MGB models, which have
self-adjusting discs (see later) at the front.

Disc-braked Models

Twin-Cam Model.—The Dunlop fully disc-braked Twin-
Cam sports cars have no brake adjustment all—as the pads
wear down the clearance is taken up each time the pedal is
depressed by the caliper pistons. The correct amount of pedal
free travel is set during manufacture, but if this is disturbed it
must be re-set correctly to make sure the master-cylinder
piston is not under load when the pedal is fully off.

With the pedal in this position, the piston must be held
against the dished washer at the head of the master-cylinder
bore by the pressure of the return spring, thus forming a return
stop. Free end-play of 0·015–0·020 in. should be felt at the
master-cylinder push rod. If necessary, the length of the push
rod can be altered to achieve this clearance.

Front Disc Brakes of 1100, MGA 1600 and MGB Models.—
These Lockheed disc brakes also require no regular adjustment. On each brake application, the disc pads come into con-

1. Caliper.
2. Cylinder block.
3. Cylinder block.
4. Bridge pipe.
5. Keep plate.
6. Support plate.
7. Friction pad.
8. Securing plate.
9. Backing plate.
10. Dust seal.
11. Piston.
12. Piston seal.
13. Retractor bush.
14. Plate.
15. Cap.
16. Spring washer.
17. Retractor stop bush.
18. Retractor pin.
19. Bleed screw.
20. Bleed screw ball.

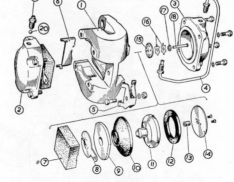

FIG. 58.—COMPONENT PARTS OF DUNLOP DISC BRAKES USED ON TWIN CAM

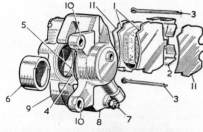

FIG. 59 (above).—COMPONENT PARTS OF LOCKHEED DISC-BRAKE CALIPER FITTED TO 1100

1. Friction Pads.
2. Pad retaining spring.
3. Retaining pin.
4. Piston dust seal.
5. Piston fluid seal.
6. Piston
7. Bleeder screw.
8. Caliper (mounting half).
9. Caliper (rim half).
10. Caliper mounting point.
11. Anti-squeak shims.

FIG. 60 (below).—ASSEMBLED VIEW OF 1100 FRONT DISC BRAKE

1. Brake disc.
2. Bleeder screw.
3. Caliper assembly.

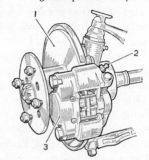

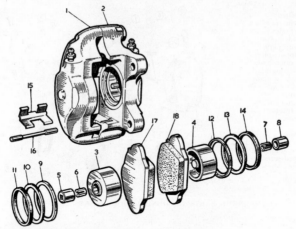

FIG. 61.—LOCKHEED DISC BRAKE CALIPER COMPONENTS ON MGA 1600 MODELS

1. Caliper—rim half.	11. Fluid seal.
2. Caliper—mounting half.	12. Dust seal retainer.
3. and 4. Hydraulic pistons.	13. Dust seal.
5. Sleeve.	14. Fluid seal.
6. and 7. Friction stops.	15. Retainer spring.
8. Sleeve.	16. Retainer pin.
9. Dust seal retainer.	17. and 18. Friction pads.
10. Dust seal.	

tact with the discs, providing the necessary retardation, and when the pedal pressure is released the caliper pistons draw the pads off the discs just enough to give a running clearance. This is achieved by means of a rubber lip-ring that fits around the edge of the caliper bore, for as the piston moves out the ring is partially displaced and when the pressure drops the rubber draws the piston back into the bore.

Every 6,000 miles the pad-lining wear should be checked, for they do not last as long as brake-shoe linings, and when there is only about $\frac{1}{16}$ in. of lining left they should be changed. This is quite a simple procedure that involves jacking up the front of the car and removing the road wheels. The two large split pins can be withdrawn from the rear of the caliper assembly and the retaining spring over the pads lifted out. Use a pair of pliers to draw out the two pads from each side of the caliper, bringing with them any shims that might also be present.

The caliper pistons must then be levered back into the caliper bores to make room for the newly-lined pads to be fitted; before doing this remove the top of the master-cylinder reservoir as a certain amount of fluid will be forced back into it. With the new pads fitted and the springs and split pins in place, the brake pedal should be pumped a few times to adjust the pads up to the discs.

Fitting Relined Shoes

The fitting of relined shoes to drum-brake systems is quite straightforward, providing the positions of the shoe-return springs is noted before the old shoes are taken off. With the new shoes in place, the adjusters should be let right off to make the refitting of the drums as easy as possible.

Always clean the back-plates when relining brakes, and make sure in the case of the rear units that the floating wheel cylinders are free to slide and not partially seized. Never depress the brake pedal with the drum off, or the wheel cylinders will have their insides forced out under the fluid pressure. With the brakes assembled, they can be adjusted in the normal way and after a short period of running they should be bedded-in and can be adjusted again.

Bleeding the System

Since air is readily compressible, it has no place in the hydraulic system for it causes 'spongy' braking. Therefore, whenever the fluid system is opened to the air, or a leak occurs, upon reassembly the first thing that has to be done is the removal of any air from the fluid in the system. This applies to both drum and disc brakes, for where the bleed screws are to be found on the back plates of drum brakes, there is also one on each caliper unit of disc brakes.

To bleed the brakes, the reservoir must be topped up and kept at least half full throughout the operation. Starting at the bleed screw nearest the master cylinder, attach a piece of pipe to the bleed nipple and let it hang into a glass jar containing more clean fluid. Slacken the bleed screw a turn and have an

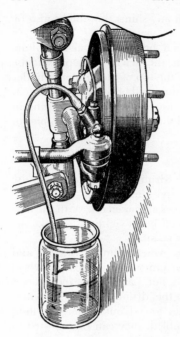

FIG. 62 (*left*).—BLEEDING HYDRAULIC BRAKES

The special bleeding tube in use in conjunction with a glass jar to clear the system of air.

FIG. 63 (*below*).—HANDBRAKE CARRIER COMPONENTS OF MGA TWIN CAM

1. Outer pad carrier.
2. Inner pad carrier.
3. Pads.
4. Lever.
5. Adjuster bolt.
6. Locknut.
7. Trunnion.
8. Pivot pin.
9. Pivot seat.
10. Spring.
11. Spring retaining nut.
12. Spring plate.

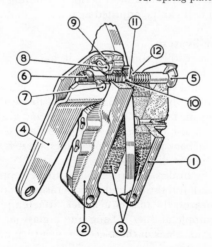

assistant slowly pump the brake pedal down a number of times, until the fluid that can be seen coming from the pipe is free of air bubbles. When this point is reached tell the assistant to hold the brake pedal *down* on the next stroke and when it is held in this position tighten the bleed screw.

This action has to be repeated at each bleed screw, working away from the master cylinder. Top up the reservoir each time with clean fluid, not the fluid from the jar as this will contain air; this fluid must be left at least 24 hours before it is used again.

Handbrake

In all cases the handbrake only operates the rear wheels of the car and from the handbrake lever sheathed cables run to the arms on the rear back-plates. Normally, the handbrake is adjusted at the same time as the shoes are adjusted in the manner described earlier, but sometimes parts wear and cables stretch and the handbrake requires some separate adjustment.

On all models with a floor-mounted lever, the cables can be seen at the base of the lever, the screwed ends of the cables having nuts on them; by screwing the nuts on further the cables are tightened. Where a fascia-mounted pistol-grip type of lever is employed there are adjusting nuts for the cables under the car on the cross-lever.

Handbrakes should always be adjusted with the rear wheels jacked up and set so that the lever is up about five clicks and both the rear wheels are *just* locked. They might be able to be turned with very stiff resistance, in which case this should be equal.

WHEELS AND TYRES

Tyre pressures play an important part in braking, for too high a pressure will cut down contact with the road and assist skidding when braking in an emergency. Of course, fierce braking also affects tyre life adversely and should be avoided.

Too low a pressure in a tyre causes the side wall to bulge and will in time weaken it to such an extent that it could burst.

Always keep the tyres, including the spare, at the correct pressures and give them fairly regular examinations to remove flints and stones from the treads. To regularise tyre wear, the wheels should be changed around diagonally at 3,000-mile intervals.

Wheel Balance

On the majority of models built by M.G. since 1946, the front suspension has been of the independent type and with this suspension the balance of the wheels plays an important part in accurate steering. Perfect steering in a new car can gradually become less efficient as the wheel bearings, tyres and other components wear. This can result in quite heavy vibration on the steering wheel during a certain speed range.

If this should develop, the wheels should be balanced on a static and dynamic balancing machine, which some garages might have, but all tyre depots are sure to have. The balance is achieved by adding small weights to the rim of the wheel until it runs true, and in such a state it will cause no irregularity on the steering.

Tyres

Tubed tyres are not difficult to remove or replace, providing the tube is completely deflated and the first part of the tyre to be levered out is adjacent to the valve. New tyres should be fitted opposite to this.

All the latest models have tubeless tyres, which are more reliable as they have a lower rate of air loss and will not deflate quickly when punctured, providing the cause of the puncture is left in the tyre. Naturally, tyres should be inspected regularly and any small objects removed from the tread. If a slow puncture develops it can be traced by immersing the complete wheel in a tub of water.

Repairing Punctures

A puncture in a tubed tyre can be repaired by using a suitable patch and rubber solution after tracing the hole, but a far more reliable method is the fixing of a patch under heat to weld the two rubbers together, and this vulcanising treatment can only be carried out by a garage.

Tubeless tyre punctures can be repaired by 'plugging'. The puncture is traced and marked, then the plugging needle dipped into the solution and pushed through the hole in the tyre, repeating this operation several times until the hole is well lubricated with solution.

A plug about twice the diameter of the hole is selected and rolled into the eye of the needle about $\frac{1}{2}$ in. from its end, the plug and needle is then dipped in the solution. Push the needle through the puncture, taking with it the plug, and then withdrawn leaving the plug in the hole. Cut off the plug allowing about $\frac{1}{8}$ in. of it to protrude above the tyre tread and inflate the tyre.

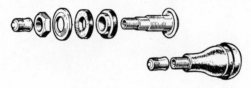

FIG. 64.—VALVES FOR TUBELESS TYRES

It is quite feasible to use an inner tube with a tubeless tyre if for any reason a repair cannot be carried out, but this should not be done where a tyre is damaged so as to leave any portion of the tube unsupported.

Removing Tubeless Tyres

The tyres themselves can be taken off a wheel in the same way as the tubed versions, that is by pushing the tread down into the wheel well before levering out the bead diametrically opposite. When using the tyre levers extreme care must be taken not to damage the bead, for it is this that makes an airtight seal with the wheel.

With the tyre removed examine the wheel and straighten any slight irregularity on the rim edge, then clean this with steel wool or emery cloth to make the seating for the tyre beading as clean as possible. Having fitted a tyre to the wheel a tourniquet of some description must be placed around the tyre tread and tightened so as to push the tyre bead out on to the rim as far as it can. Compressed air can then be passed through the valve to complete the fitting process.

Tyre Valves

There are two types of tubeless tyre valve, these being illustrated in Fig. 64. The first is made of metal and is secured to the wheel by means of a nut, sealing being carried out by two rubber washers. The other is all rubber and can be fitted by drawing it through the wheel-valve hole using a special tool. The air inside the tyre when it is inflated keeps this valve leak-proof.

CHAPTER IX

STEERING AND SUSPENSION

THE majority of M.G. cars built since the war have used rack and pinion steering systems, but the immediate post-war models and the Farina-styled Magnettes have cam-and-peg steering boxes either by Bishop Gears or Cam Gears.

Cam and Peg Steering

Basically, this type of steering box takes the form of a deep-cut thread or 'worm' on the bottom of the steering mast, this being supported in ball bearings inside a casing. A rocker shaft, passing through the side of the box, carries the lever which has a conical peg that engages in the worm. As the steering wheel is turned so does the worm, which makes the rocker shaft move through a pre-determined angle. The side lever (drop arm) attached to the rocker shaft transmits this movement, via the steering linkage to the steering arms provided at the front wheels.

Rocker-shaft Adjustment

As the steering parts wear more in the straight-ahead position, the worm is machined with greater clearance at each end than in the middle and allowance must be made for this when adjusting. The adjustment takes the form of shims under the side and bottom covers of the Bishop box, and a setscrew with locknut (14, 15, Fig. 65) passing through the top of the Cam Gears box; this adjusting screw bears down on to the rocker shaft.

Adjustment to the Bishop box can be made by removing the drag link and taking a shim away from under the side cover, thereby making the cover push the lever and peg deeper into mesh with the worm when it is screwed back in place. On the Cam Gears box, by screwing the adjuster in it bears down

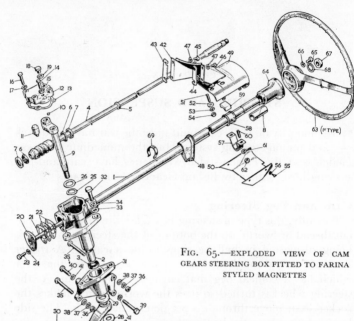

Fig. 65.—EXPLODED VIEW OF CAM GEARS STEERING BOX FITTED TO FARINA STYLED MAGNETTES

1. Box and outer column.
2. Rocker-shaft bush.
3. Rocker shaft seal.
4. Column with cam (inner).
5. Ring (rubber).
6. Cage assembly—ball.
7. Cup for ball cage.
8. Bush (felt).
9. Rocker shaft (with thrust disc).
10. Thrust disc.
11. Cam roller assembly.
12. Side cover.
13. Joint for side cover.
14. Thrust screw.
15. Nut for screw (lock).
16. Bolt for side cover.
17. Washer for bolt (spring).
18. Oil plug.
19. Washer for plug.
20. End cover (with stator tube).
21. Joint for cover.
22. Shim.
23. Bolt for end cover.

24. Washer for bolt (spring).
25. Washer (bent).
26. Washer (retaining).
27. Nut—lever to steering gear.
28. Washer for nut (plain).
29. Dust seal.
30. Side lever.
31. Steering box bracket.
32. Steering-box to bracket bolt.
33. Washer for bolt (plain).
34. Washer for bolt (spring).
35. Bracket to frame bolt.
36. Nut for bolt.
37. Washer for bolt (spring).
38. Washer for bolt (plain).
39. Bracket to body bolt.
40. Screw—bracket to body.
41. Washer for screw (spring).
42. Bracket support—steering column.
43. Distance plate.
44. Distance plate.
45. Bracket screw.

46. Bracket screw.
47. Washer for screw (spring).
48. Steering-column grommet.
49. Cover assembly (upper).
50. Cover assembly (lower).
51. Stud—cover to bracket.
52. Washer for stud (plain).
53. Washer for stud (spring).
54. Nut for stud.
55. Screw—lower to upper cover.
56. Washer (spring).
57. Clip—steering-column.
58. Packing piece.
59. Distance piece.
60. Stud—clip to column.
61. Washer for stud (spring).
62. Nut for stud.
63. Steering wheel.
64. Steering-wheel hub.
65. Screw—wheel to hub.
66. Washer for screw (spring).
67. Nut for steering-wheel.
68. Washer for nut (shake-proof).
69. Dust seal.

harder and pushes the conical peg deeper into mesh with the worm, thereby taking up any play.

On the Cam Gears box, the backlash can be adjusted with the steering box fitted to the car and the front wheels jacked up off the ground, but with the drag link disconnected. The adjuster must be screwed into the box until there is no free play on the drop arm with the steering in the straight-ahead position, but be careful not to over-tighten the adjuster.

To check for free play, hold the steering wheel still while an assistant moves the drop arm back and forth; the correct setting is when there is no backlash on carrying out this test.

Steering Column End-float Adjustment

With both boxes, should end-float be present on the steering mast, the box will have to be taken from the car completely so that the bottom cover can be removed and a shim (22, Fig. 65), extracted; this will diminish any end-float.

RACK AND PINION STEERING

A housing is attached to the underside of the car bulkhead through the centre of which runs the rack—this being a round steel bar with teeth machined along one side for part of its length. These teeth are hardened by heating to resist wear. Meshing with the rack teeth is a pinion gear which has a splined shaft that is connected to the bottom of the steering column. Therefore, as the steering wheel is turned so is the pinion gear and this moves the rack along its housing.

The rack is slightly 'loaded' against the pinion by means of an adjustable damper let into the underside of the rack housing. The damper assembly consists of a pad which bears against the rack and keeps it in close mesh with the pinion, a spring, and a shim-packed housing. These shims offer a means of adjustment, for if one or more is removed it alters the pressure of the spring on the damper pad. Some models have a second damper at the other end of the rack housing, but this is non-adjustable.

The pinion is supported in the rack housing by hardened steel washers above and below it to prevent wear. Under the

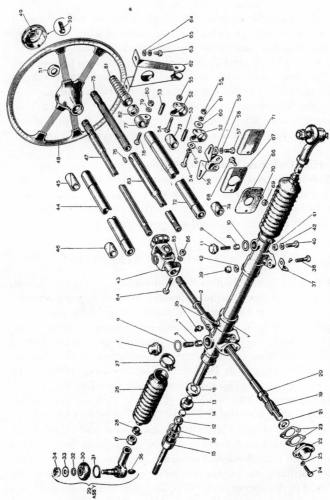

FIG. 66.—EXPLODED VIEW OF TYPICAL RACK-AND-PINION STEERING LAYOUT
This is as used on MGA models. For key to numbers, see facing page.

1. Rack-housing assembly.
2. Pinion-shaft seal.
3. Steering rack.
4. Rack damper pad.
5. Rack damper spring.
6. Pad housing shim.
7. Rack damper housing.
8. Rack-damper secondary pad.
9. Rack-damper secondary spring.
10. Rack-damper secondary washer.
11. Rack-damper secondary housing.
12. Tie rod.
13. Male ball housing.
14. Ball seat.
15. Female ball housing.
16. Ball-housing shim.
17. Tie-rod lock-nut.
18. Tie-rod lock-washer.
19. Steering pinion.
20. Upper pinion thrust washer.
21. Lower pinion thrust washer.
22. Pinion tail bearing.
23. Tail bearing shim.
24. Bearing to steering box screw.
25. Bearing screw spring washer.
26. Rack seal.
27. Large seal-clip assembly.
28. Small seal-clip assembly.
29. Ball-socket assembly.
30. Rubber boot.

31. Boot clip.
32. Boot-clip ring.
33. Ball-socket washer.
34. Ball-socket nut.
35. Pinion/rack greaser.
36. Ball socket greaser.
37. Steering-rack to brackets shim.
38. Rack to bracket (front) bolt.
39. Rack to bracket (Nylon) nut.
40. Rack to bracket (rear) bolt.
41. Rack to bracket (rear) nut.
42. Rack to bracket spring washer.
43. Steering-column universal joint.
44. Outer tube.
45. Upper end felt bush.
46. Lower end felt bush.
47. Inner tube assembly.
48. Steering-wheel.
49. Steering-wheel cover.
50. Cover-spring clip.
51. Steering-wheel nut.
52. Steering-column clamp.
53. Clamp distance-piece.
54. Clamp bolt.
55. Clamp-bolt nut.
56. Steering-column bracket (lower).
57. Bracket to frame screw.
58. Bracket to frame spring washer.
59. Bracket to frame plain washer.

60. Lower bracket to clamp plain washer.
61. Lower bracket to clamp spring washer.
62. Steering-column upper bracket.
63. Bracket to body rail screw.
64. Plain washer.
65. Spring washer.
66. Column rubber seal.
67. Column seal retainer.
68. Seal and retainer to dash screw.
69. Seal/retainer screw nut.
70. Seal/retainer screw spring washer.
71. Blanking plate.
72. Column outer tube.
73. Upper bush.
74. Lower bush.
75. Adjustable top end.
76. Top end key.
77. Collar clamp.
78. Clamp bolt.
79. Clamp-bolt spring washer.
80. Clamp-bolt nut.
81. Spring cover.
82. Spring-cover cup.
83. Inner-tube assembly.
84. Universal-joint bolt.
85. Spring washer.
86. Universal-joint bolt nut.

pinion a diamond-shaped casing bolted to the rack housing is fitted with shims so that the pinion end-float can be controlled.

At each outer end of the rack a ball-joint connects a tie-rod with an adjustable end to the steering arms on the front hubs, thereby providing the push-pull movement required to operate the road wheels. At this point, each end of the rack housing has a rubber gaiter fitted over it to ensure that no lubricant leaks out, the gaiters being secured by screw clips.

Rack and Pinion Lubrication

As both the rack and pinion move in plain bearings, adequate lubrication is required and it is recommended that a hypoid oil be used. On no account should the rack be over-lubricated, for on turning the steering suddenly from side-to-side the excess oil will build-up in one gaiter and exert enough pressure to burst it, allowing oil to leak away and dirt to enter the rack housing.

Some models have a lubricating nipple for the steering rack that can be reached either from under the car or through an access hole in the floorboards ahead of the passengers seat. This nipple should be given about six strokes with a grease-gun filled with SAE 90 hypoid oil every 12,000 miles. The 1100 is filled with lubricant and this lasts the life of the unit, unless a gaiter should fail and let it leak away. If this happens, rack filling is achieved by undoing the hose clip on the nearside gaiter, peeling it back off the rack housing, and injecting the required quantity of oil.

Rack and Pinion Adjustment—except 1100 and MGB

The most common adjustment will be to the rack damper to overcome steering rattle and shake. To do this, the damper housing must be taken off and the pad, spring and shims removed; refit the pad to the housing and bolt this back up to the rack, tightening it until it is just possible to pull the rack through its casing. Measure the gap between the rack and damper housings with feeler gauges and add to the figure obtained between 0·002 and 0·005 in. This will give the thickness of shims required and as they are available in only one size, 0·003 in., this is the figure that must be worked to.

When the number of shims has been ascertained, the damper housing is taken off, the spring refitted under the pad and the shims placed under the housing before it is bolted back in position. On racks having two dampers, the above operation to the adjustable one must be carried out with the other in position, and should the non-adjustable pad be removed at any time it has to be replaced as it was before, with the fibre washer and packing washer in their correct position.

The end-float of the pinion should be 0·002–0·005 in. and is adjusted by shims (23), Fig. 66.

If a rack has been taken out for overhaul, the assembly setting-up procedure is the same as above, but also the tie-rod ball joints on the end of the rack have to be correctly fitted. To do this, the tie-rod has to be attached to the rack with no shims and the ball-joint casing tightened up as far as it will go; the joint has to be reasonably tight with no slackness in any position. If it is too tight, fit shims under the casing until the right tightness is achieved. Shims for this adjustment are available in 0·002 in., 0·003 and 0·005 in. thicknesses.

Normally, the rack and pinion will give no trouble for extremely long periods, if of course, the correct lubrication is carried out and no dirt is allowed to enter the rack housing.

Rack and Pinion Adjustment—1100 Model

To adjust or overhaul the steering gear it has to be removed.

Pinion end-play is eliminated and a preload of 0·002 in. is given to the pinion thrust-bearings by adjustment of shims beneath the pinion-bearing-retaining cover. See (A), Fig. 67.

To obtain the required 0·002 in. preload, remove the rack support cover and place the pinion-bearing cover in position without the shims and paper joint and without over-tightening the cover screws (20 lb. load). The clearance between the cover and the housing is then measured with a feeler gauge. Shims and a new paper joint are then fitted in position to the thickness measured minus 0·002 in. Before final assembly, the joint face of the housing and the bolts must be coated with jointing compound to prevent leakage of lubricant from the housing. The pinion should revolve freely without shake, although the rack is unsupported.

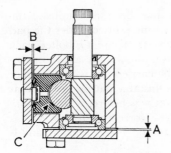

FIG. 67.—SECTION THROUGH
STEERING PINION AND RACK
DAMPER ON 1100

During adjustment feeler-
gauge measurements at (A) and
(B) must be taken without
packing shims fitted. (C) is the
damper yoke.

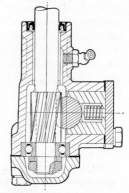

FIG. 68.—SECTION
THROUGH STEERING PINION
AND RACK DAMPER ON
MGB

A spring-loaded pad or yoke behind the steering rack and
packing shims between the housing and rack-support cover
control the backlash between the pinion and rack. To adjust,
the cover plate is fitted without the shims and Belleville spring
washers. Lightly tighten the two cover-securing bolts until they
are just nipped, with the rack in the straight-ahead position.
Measure the gap between the cover and the rack housing. See
(B), Fig. 67. Remove the cover, apply jointing compound to
the joint face and bolts, and refit the cover with spring and
packing shims, the thickness of the packing shims and new
paper joint being equal to feeler-gauge thickness plus 0·006 in.

Rack and Pinion Adjustment—MGB

No adjustment is required to pinion ball bearing. The outer
edge of the ball-race locknut must be peened into the slot in
the pinion shaft if removed and refitted.

To adjust the rack damper, replace the plunger in the
housing and tighten down cover without spring or shims until
it is just possible to rotate the pinion shaft by drawing the rack
through the housing. Measure the gap between the cover and
the rack housing. See Fig. 68. Remove the cover and plunger,

apply jointing compound to the joint face and bolts, and refit the plunger (with spring), cover and packing shims, the thickness of the packing shims and new paper joint being equal to feeler-gauge thickness plus 0·005–0·003 in.

SOLID-AXLE FRONT SUSPENSION

This non-independent front-suspension layout, used on the TC Midget (1946–9), takes the form of a solid beam across the front of the car, it being attached to the chassis by two leaf-type springs with shackles at each end; these springs are of the semi-elliptic variety.

With this suspension, the steering movement at the front wheels is made possible by means of stub-axles through which pass swivel pins running in bushes, the swivel pin fitting through the top eye of the stub-axle, then through the main-axle beam, and on through the lower eye of the stub-axle. A steering arm is attached to each stub-axle and attached to these are the ends of the steering track rods.

There is little maintenance required, apart from periodic oiling of the front springs and greasing the shackles. It is advisable to check the tightness of the spring 'U' bolts now and then. Should a spring or front axle be removed, make a note of the way the wedges (if any) are fitted between the springs and the axle, for these control the caster angle.

INDEPENDENT FRONT SUSPENSION

Except for the Hydrolastic suspensioned 1100, dealt with later, the independent suspension models use unequal-length wishbones and coil springs, in many cases the upper-suspension wishbone also serves as the operating arm for the front shock absorbers.

To remove a coil spring, the front of the car has to be jacked up and a coil-spring compressing tool used to hold the spring in compression while the bolts holding the spring plate to the lower-suspension wishbone are removed. The spring tension can be gradually released until it is free.

The front arm of the upper-suspension wishbone is fixed at its inner end to the shock-absorber spindle by a clamp bolt; to

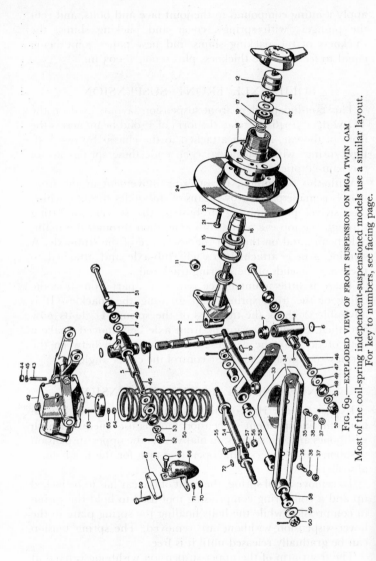

FIG. 69.—EXPLODED VIEW OF FRONT SUSPENSION ON MGA TWIN CAM.
Most of the coil-spring independent-suspensioned models use a similar layout.
For key to numbers, see facing page.

1. Steering knuckle (left-hand).
2. Swivel pin (left-hand).
3. Upper swivel pin (left-hand).
4. Swivel pin link (left-hand).
5. Bush.
6. Plate.
7. Swivel pin seal.
8. Link grease nipple.
9. Steering lever (left-hand.)
10. Steering lever key.
11. Nut for steering lever.
12. Grease-retaining cup.
13. Hub distance washer.
14. Hub oil seal.
15. Large hub bearing.
16. Hub bearing distance piece.
17. Small hub bearing.
18. Front hub assembly.
19. Bearing adjustment shims.
21. Bolt for brake disc mounting.
23. Spring washer for disc mounting bolt.
24. Disc brake.
33. Spring pan assembly.
34. Bottom wishbone assembly.
35 and 36. Spring pan to wishbone screw.
37. Spring pan to wishbone screw nut.
38. Pan to wishbone screw spring washer.
40. Washer.
41. Nut (left-hand thread).
42. Hydraulic damper.
43. Hydraulic damper to cross-member stud.
44. Hydraulic damper to cross-member stud nut.
45. Hydraulic damper to cross-member spring washer.
46. Link distance tube.
47. Link thrust washer.
48. Link seal.
49. Link seal support.
50. Coil spring.
51. Wishbone to link bolt.
52. Wishbone to link castle nut.
53. Wishbone to link spring washer.
54. Wishbone pivot.
55. Pivot to member bolt.
56. Pivot to member bolt nut.
57. Pivot to member bolt spring washer.
58. Bush for bottom wishbone.
59. Washer for wishbone pivot.
60. Slotted nut for wishbone pivot.
61. Bottom wishbone to link bolt.
62. Spring spigot.
63. Spigot to member screw.
64. Spigot to member screw nut.
65. Spigot member screw washer.
66. Check rubber.
67. Check rubber distance piece.
68. Check rubber to member screw.
69. Check rubber to member bolt.
70. Nut.
71. Spring washer.
72. Plain washer.

withdraw the top outer-pivot pin, this clamp bolt has to be slackened so that the arm can be partially withdrawn; the pivot pin can then be extracted and after releasing the shock absorber it can be removed complete with the top wishbone.

On the Farina Magnettes, the free length of the coil spring should be $11\frac{11}{16}$ in. and there is no adjustment to springs not conforming to this measurement. Early models may have a packing piece under the coil spring, and when fitting a new spring leave out the packing piece and make sure that the latest spring, Part No. 11H 53, which is the correct length to make up for the difference the packings make, is fitted.

When servicing independent front suspensions it must be pointed out that a very full range of tools is required, as well as certain special tools without which the correct setting-up of the suspension cannot be achieved. Should the suspension be put together incorrectly it will of course affect all the steering geometry and lead to advance wear on parts and tyres.

REAR-SUSPENSION ASSEMBLIES

The only car in the M.G. range since the war to have independent rear suspension is the 1100, the complete suspension of which is dealt with below. All other models have solid rear axles mounted to the sub-frame or chassis by semi-elliptic leaf springs with one solid and one swinging shackle.

Springs that have rubber inserts between the leaves and rubber shackle bushes should not be lubricated with paraffin or oil; if they become 'squeaky' treat the rubber with a liberal amount of brake fluid or rubber lubricant. Earlier models with no inserts and plain metal bushes can be lubricated with oil.

The removal and replacement of the springs is quite straightforward, and all that need be remembered is that on assembling drop the car to the ground before the shackle bolts are fully tightened as the rubber bushes are then flexed correctly.

HYDROLASTIC SUSPENSION—1100 MODEL

The rubber/fluid suspension medium of the 1100 is very novel and has received much acclaim by all concerned with

FIG. 70.—M.G. 1100 FRONT SUB-FRAME WITH BRAKES AND HYDROLASTIC SUS-
PENSION ASSEMBLED

modern motor engineering. At the front, unequal-length wishbones again carry the swivel-hub assemblies, but the springing
is by a rubber-cone unit with metal inserts bonded to its
sides. Across the base of the cone fits a flexible diaphragm, and
in the space thus achieved water is introduced under pressure.

At the rear, long trailing arms carry the stub-axles and the
rubber cone units are situated on their sides. Each unit (there
are four on each car) is inter-connected front-to-rear on the
sides of the car and there is no connection whatsoever across
the vehicle. The Hydrolastic units (as they are called) thereby
offer a suspension that cuts down vehicle pitching to a minimum and decreases body roll on corners.

Front Suspension (Hydrolastic)

The upper and lower wishbones on each side are mounted at their inner ends to the side-members of the sub-frame, while through their outer ends pass ball joints attached to the swivel-hub mast. A socket in the top of the upper wishbone carries the ball-end of a short trumpet strut, the other end of which bears against the underside of the Hydrolastic unit.

Whilst the front-swivel-hub mast can be removed, as well as the drive shafts, with little difficulty, to take out a Hydrolastic spring unit, the system on that side has to be depressurised. This can only be carried out using the B.M.C. Hydrolastic Suspension Service Unit, and this piece of equipment has to be used for completely evacuating the system and making pressure changes and checks.

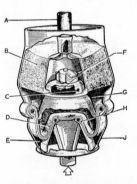

Fig. 71.—SECTION THROUGH A HYDROLASTIC UNIT

A. Interconnecting pipe.
B. Rubber spring.
C. Damper bleed.
D. Butyl liner.
E. Tapered piston
F. Damper valves.
G. Fluid-separating member.
H. Rubber diaphragm (nylon-reinforced).
J. Tapered cylinder.

To dismantle the front suspension, clip on the Service Unit and depressurise the system, then disconnect the pipe at the top of the Hydrolastic spring unit. Take off the upper wishbone completely by withdrawing the inner-pivot pin and the suspension unit can then be removed from the sub-frame tower.

When refitting the suspension, pack the top-wishbone inner bearings with molybdenum grease and make sure the torque required to move the arm is between 5 and 10 lb.–in.; this can be adjusted by using a different spacer on the pivot pin, the normal one being 0·301 in. thick. With everything in

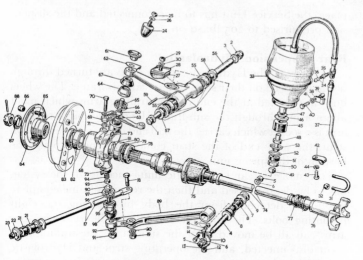

Fig. 72.—1100 FRONT SUSPENSION, HUB AND DRIVE-SHAFT ASSEMBLY

1. Upper-arm pivot pin.
2. Pivot-pin nut.
3. Plain washer.
4. Lower-arm pivot pin.
5. Pivot-pin nut.
6. Spring washer.
7. Plain washer.
8. Lower-arm bush.
9. Locating bush.
10. Retaining plate (L.H. and R.H.).
11. Retaining-plate bolt.
12. Nut.
13. Spring washer.
14. Bolt.
15. Nut.
16. Spring washer.
17. Tie-rod.
18. Tie-rod bolt.
19. Nut.
20. Spring washer.
21. Pad.
22. Cup washer.
23. Tie-rod nut.
24. Bump rubber.
25. Nut.
26. Spring washer.
27. Rebound buffer.
28. Lockwasher.
29. Nut.
30. Spring washer.
31. 'U' bolt.
32. Nut.
33. Displacer unit.
34. Valve assembly.
35. Valve core.

36. Valve cap.
37. Interconnecting pipe (L.H. and R.H.).
38. Clip.
39. Distance piece.
40. Screw.
41. Spring washer.
42. Clip.
43. Screw.
44. Washer.
45. Roller-joint seal.
46. Washer.
47. Washer.
48. Foot-roller joint.
49. Roller-joint seat.
50. Locating bush.
51. Retaining pad.
52. Retaining bush.
53. Circlip.
54. Upper-arm support assembly (L.H. and R.H.).
55. Pivot-shaft bearing.
56. Pivot tube.
57. Distance collar.
58. Spacer.
59. Locking pin.
60. Upper ball pin.
61. Nut with bumper cup.
62. Lock washer.
63. Ball seat.
64. Ball-pin retainer.
65. Ball-pin shim.
66. Lockwasher.
67. Dust cover.

68. Swivel hub (L.H. and R.H.).
69. Steering-arm (L.H. and R.H.).
70. Bolt.
71. Dowel.
72. Lock washer.
73. Lubricator.
74. Drive-shaft assembly (L.H. and R.H.).
75. Rubber boot.
76. Flange.
77. Seal.
78. Inner oil seal.
79. Spacer.
80. Inner bearing.
81. Distance piece.
82. Outer bearing.
83. Outer oil seal.
84. Driving flange.
85. Wheel stud.
86. Wheel nut.
87. Drive-shaft collar.
88. Drive-shaft nut.
89. Lower-support arm (L.H. and R.H.).
90. Lower-ball pin.
91. Nut.
92. Spring washer.
93. Ball seat.
94. Spring.
95. Retainer.
96. Shim.
97. Lock washer.
98. Dust cover.

place, the Service Unit has to be reconnected and the suspension pressurised to 205 lb./sq. in.

Rear Suspension (Hydrolastic)

At the rear, the Hydrolastic spring units are turned through 90° and placed on their sides in the rear sub-frame. The wheel hubs are carried at the end of long trailing arms which pivot about a pin through the sub-frame. Under the pivot on each arm is a socket which carries the ball end of the rear-suspension strut, the wide end of the strut comes into contact with the bottom of the spring unit.

To remove a rear Hydrolastic unit, once again the system has to be depressurised and then the rear sub-frame complete has to be detached from the body by undoing the eight mounting bolts. The anti-roll bar and two short torsion-bar arms can all be moved from the sub-frame, the trailing-arm pivot disconnected, and the operating strut and Hydrolastic unit lifted out.

Hubs

The front hubs are all part of the complete swivel-unit mast and this can be removed by disconnecting the inner drive-shaft joints and also the ends of the steering rack from the arms on the hubs. Remove the brake pipes from the calipers and disconnect the upper and lower wishbones from the ball joints at the top and bottom of the swivel mast. Push out the inner-pivot pin on the lower wishbone and the complete hub and swivel-mast assembly, brakes, drive shaft, and lower wishbone can be removed from the car and dismantled on the bench.

The rear hubs are cast with the brake drums and to remove this assembly, prise out the grease-retaining cap so that the hub nut can be undone. The hub can then be drawn off the stub axle using a suitable drawer.

Hydrolastic Suspension Heights

If at any time it seems that the Hydrolastic suspension is down on one side it should be taken to an M.G. dealer so the pressure can be checked. However, before doing this, the owner, as a guide, can measure the distance between the centre of the road wheel and the bottom edge of the body wing directly above this point.

With the car on level ground and having its correct amount of oil, water and four gallons of fuel, and with the proper suspension pressure of 205 lb./sq. in. the measurement should be $13\frac{5}{8}$ in. plus or minus $\frac{1}{4}$ in. If a Hydrolastic suspension unit should become faulty, the suspension is so designed that it will not collapse; all that happens is that the suspension arms will come up into contact with the bump rubbers and the car can be driven in this condition on good-surfaced roads providing 30 m.p.h. is not exceeded and the suspension is repaired as quickly as possible.

When fitting a new Hydrolastic unit, the system has to be pressurised to 350 lb./sq. in. on that side for a period of 20 mins., then let down to the correct pressure of 205 lb./sq. in.

E

CHAPTER X

REAR AXLE

Two types of rear axle have been fitted to M.G. cars since 1946: Midgets TD, TF and YB Saloon have a semi-floating type, while all others employ a three-quarter floating axle with spiral-bevel final drive on Midget TC and Y Saloon and hypoid gears on all other models. The front-wheel drive 1100 has its differential in the power unit/transmission casing and this can be dealt with separately.

The main difference between the two types of axle is that in the semi-floating unit, the half-shaft is not only subjected to torque, but also to sheer stresses as it supports the hub and brake drum. With the three-quarter floating axle, the half-shafts are only subjected to torque as they transmit the drive. Recognition is also easy, for the semi-floating axles are fitted with split casings in two halves, the join being around the differential housing. Three-quarter floating axles have a one-piece axle casing, the differential can be removed from the front of this casing after undoing a series of nuts around the differential carrier.

The very latest MGB models have rear axles of the three-quarter floating type, but without removable differentials. There is a cover over the back of the axle case so access can be gained to the differential with the axle in position, but for any dismantling of the differential, the complete axle has to be taken off the car.

SEMI-FLOATING AXLE

Hypoid final-drive gears are used in this axle, which provides for a large pinion gear and leads to quite silent running, providing *only* hypoid oils of the correct grade are used as lubricant. The gasket between the two halves of the axle casing is quite critical and must be the correct one, otherwise gear meshing is affected.

Pinion Assembly

Housed in the right-hand side of the axle casing is the pinion assembly, the casing being machined to take the pinion-bearing outer races, the bearings which support the pinion being of the taper-roller variety. The machined registers against which the outer races fit are a specified distance apart and virtually no machining tolerance is allowed at this point. Since the distance between the outer races is thus pre-determined, it is logical to say that the distance between the inner races must also be constant, where perfectly similar and standard thicknesses of bearing are used. This type of bearing varies to some extent in overall thickness, i.e. from the inner face of the outer race to the outer face of the inner race. To compensate for these variations, the spacer between the bearings is carefully matched for each pair.

This matching takes place at the factory and to guard against the possibility of the bearings having too much or too little pre-load, the complete assembly is supplied as a unit and should only be fitted to an axle as such. The spacers are not interchangeable and cannot be supplied separately from the bearings.

The length of the distance piece determines the amount of pre-load on the bearings and increasing the length will reduce the pre-load, while reducing the length will cause it to be increased. The desired pre-load is between 11 and 13 lb.-in. A distance washer is fitted against the pinion head and by varying the thickness of this washer the pinion setting position alters; there is a range of different sized washers to provide this adjustment.

The order of assembly of the pinion is as follows: pinion, pinion-head washer, pinion bearing and spacer assembly, oil seal, universal-joint flange, a plain washer and the securing nut. The pinion oil-seal bears down on the machined surface of the universal-joint flange.

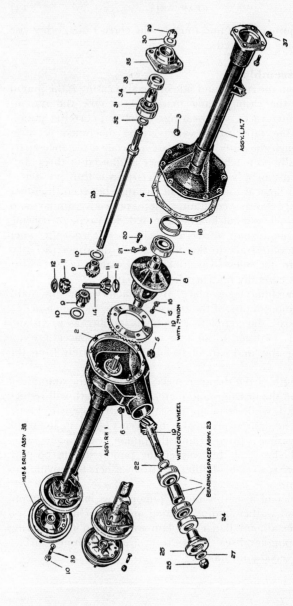

FIG. 73.—EXPLODED VIEW OF HYPOID, SEMI-FLOATING, REAR-AXLE ASSEMBLY USED ON EARLY MIDGETS TD, TF AND YB SALOON

For key to numbers, see facing page.

1. Right-hand axle-tube assembly.
2. Cover stud.
3. Axle-cover stud nut.
4. Joint.
5. Drain plug.
6. Oil-filler plug.
7. Left-hand axle-tube assembly.
8. Differential cage.
9. Differential gear.
10. Gear washer.
11. Differential pinion.
12. Pinion washer.
14. Pinion pin.
15. Pinion pin locking-bolt.
16. Locking-bolt tab washer.
17. Differential bearing.
18. Bearing distance collar.
19. Crown wheel and pinion.
20. Crown-wheel bolt.
21. Crown-wheel-bolt locking-tab.
22. Rear pinion distance washer.
23. Bearing and spacer assembly.
24. Front-pinion oil seal.
25. Universal-joint flange.
26. Pinion castle nut.
27. Castle-nut washer.
28. Rear-axle shaft.
29. Axle-shaft nut.
30. Axle-shaft nut washer.
31. Rear-hub bearing.
32. Hub-bearing distance washer.
33. Hub oil seal.
34. Oil-seal collar.
35. Brake-plate support.
37. Nut.
38. Hub and brake-drum assembly.
39. Wheel stud.
40. Wheel-stud nut.

Differential Assembly

The differential-cage assembly is supported by two deep-groove ball bearings in the two halves of the axle casing and it comprises the crownwheel and the differential planet gears on their shafts; these planet gears (or differential pinions) are secured by means of a pin and thrust washers to the differential cage.

Differential-carrier bearings are of the controlled-width type and behind each bearing, i.e. between the bearing and the machining of the axle case, a distance collar is fitted. These collars are available in different thicknesses and by selecting suitable collars, the appropriate thickness will be achieved to hold the cage rigidly in position when the two halves of the axle case are bolted together. By varying the thicknesses on each side it can be seen that the crownwheel and differential-cage assembly will move across its position inside the case, thereby providing the second main adjustment of the differential—the meshing of the crownwheel and pinion teeth.

Assembling Differential and Pinion

Always assemble the pinion to the casing first. To decide upon the thickness of the pinion-head washer when fitting a new pinion a special dummy pinion shaft is required, whilst if there is a figure marked on the head of the new pinion this also has to be taken into account. For example, if, with the dummy pinion in place, the necessary washer is 0·123 in., yet the pinion head carries no marking, this washer can be used; however, if the pinion head carries a mark −4 or −·004, then the correct washer is one 0·127 in. thick. Conversely, if the head of the new pinion carries a + sign, subtract this figure from the washer size fitting the gap of the dummy pinion and bearing to obtain the correct size of washer.

Once the correct washer has been selected, the pinion has to be assembled by first fitting the bearing outer races to the casing, and then putting the other parts in according to the order given under the heading 'Pinion Assembly'. Tighten the pinion-flange nut to a torque figure of 900 lb.–in.

When fitting the differential cage to the casing, if the same parts are used then the adjusting washers remain the same, but if new bearings or crownwheel and pinion are being used then some calculation is necessary. For example, if the marking on the side of the old crownwheel is −2 or −·002, and the marking on the new one is 0 or it carries no marking at all, then the difference is 0·002 in. To reassemble correctly a washer that is 0·002 in. *thicker* must be fitted to the large side of the axle casing and a washer 0·002 in. *thinner* fitted to the small side of the casing. The markings on the crownwheels vary from plus 2 to minus 2, those which are standard being marked 0 or having no mark at all.

If only the carrier bearings are being changed, providing genuine M.G. or B.M.C. spares are being used, the same distance washers can be used, as the bearings are of controlled-width and do not vary. The crownwheel and pinion gears are only supplied in matched pairs which will both have the same marking on them, and when fitting new gears it is much easier to get the new ones with the same markings as the old ones, for then the same pinion head washer and differential adjusting washers can be used.

Lubrication

The axle case is provided with filler and drain plugs and single hypoid gears are used it is important that the correct level is maintained. Hypoid oil allows very high-gear tooth loading and is therefore vital in this unit. An oil gallery cast in the casing feeds oil thrown up by the crownwheel through the pinion bearings, while between these bearings, and immediately in front of the front bearing, there are return drain passages to the oil reservoir part of the casing.

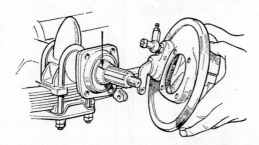

Fig. 74.—SHOWING HOW OIL-SEAL COLLAR IS PLACED ON SEMI-FLOATING AXLES WITH THE SPLIT ON A RAISED SPLINE OF THE HALF-SHAFT

Axle Shafts and Hubs

Let into the axle casing on each side is the half-shaft tube which is machined at its outer flange to accommodate the hub bearing, this being retained by the brake back-plate support flange. The axle half-shaft, supported at its inner end by the splines in the differential, is mounted in this hub bearing. Passing over the splines, and bearing hard against the inner race of the hub bearing is a tapered oil-seal collar. This serves two purposes: as well as acting as a bearing surface for the oil seal, it is also a location for the hub and brake-drum assembly, ensuring that the inner end of this is rigidly supported on the axle shaft.

When assembling the shaft and bearing-hub assembly, all parts should be perfectly clean, the oil-seal collar must be hard up against the bearing inner race when the hub/drum is

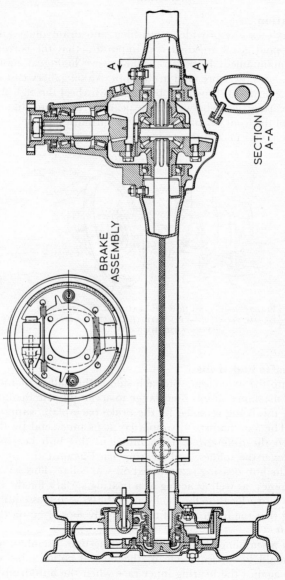

SECTION A-A

BRAKE ASSEMBLY

FIG. 75.—SECTION THROUGH B.M.C. HYPOID THREE-QUARTER FLOATING, REAR-AXLE ASSEMBLY USED ON MIDGET MK.I AND II.

fitted, and the split in the oil-seal collar should be on one of the raised splines to give it maximum rigidity.

THREE-QUARTER FLOATING AXLE

This type of axle has a detachable differential-carrier assembly that can be withdrawn from the front of the main casing. This means that the complete axle does not have to be taken from the car when any major work is required. To remove the differential, disconnect the rear end of the propeller shaft from its flange, drain the oil from the axle casing, partially withdraw the half-shafts and after undoing the nuts around the differential carrier withdraw it from the casing and place on the bench.

Setting Crownwheel and Pinion (Hypoid Gears)

Special equipment and gauges are required to make an accurate job of the differential adjustments. The differential cage is supported in two ball races which are situated in machined bores in the carrier assembly; these bores have removable caps to make the differential cage easy to detach. Within the cage are the differential pinions, these being carried by a pin which is located by a dowel. The two carrier bearings are of the thrust type and must be fitted with their thrust faces outwards. The crownwheel is bolted to the differential cage.

The pinion is situated in the carrier casing and runs in two roller bearings separated by a distance piece. Positioning of the pinion is again by a spacing washer behind the pinion head, but the correct pre-load on the bearings is obtained by shims placed between the front bearing and the distance piece.

A clock gauge is a necessity when setting the pinion in the carrier casing and the procedure is as follows.

Fit the outer races of the roller bearings into the casing and, using a spacing washer of known thickness, assemble the rear bearing on to the pinion shaft and place the pinion in the casing without the bearing spacer and oil seal. The inner race of the front bearing must now be fitted, and the driving flange replaced and tightened until the correct pre-load for the model concerned is reached.

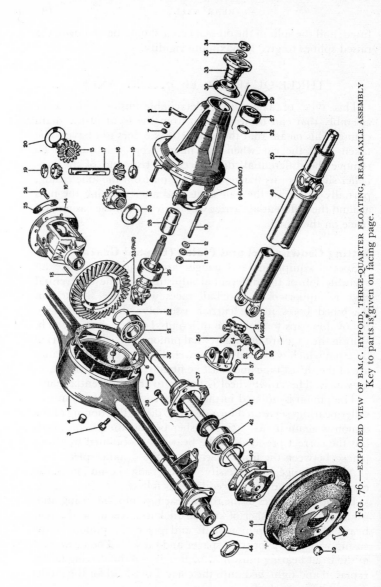

Fig. 76.—EXPLODED VIEW OF B.M.C. HYPOID, THREE-QUARTER FLOATING, REAR-AXLE ASSEMBLY

Key to parts is given on facing page.

1. Rear-axle casing
2. Differential carrier bolts.
3. Breather assembly.
4. Filler and drain plugs
5. Brake-pipe bracket.
6. Differential carrier bolt nut.
7. Spring-washer nut.
8. Joint—differential carrier to axle.
9. Carrier.
10. Cap stud.
11. Stud nut.
12. Plain washer.
13. Spring washer.
14. Differential case.
15. Differential wheel.
16. Differential pinion.
17. Pinion pin.
18. Pin-locating peg.
19. Thrust-pinion washer.
20. Thrust-wheel washer.
21. Differential bearing.
22. Bearing packing washer.
23. Crown wheel and bevel pinion.
24. Crown wheel to case bolt.
25. Bolt lock-washer.
26. Rear bevel-pinion bearing.
27. Front bevel-pinion bearing.
28. Bearings spacer.
29. Front-bearing oil seal.

30. Oil-seal dust cover.
31. Bevel-pinion washer.
32. Front bevel-pinion bearing shim.
33. Universal-joint flange.
34. Flange nut.
35. Nut spring washer.
36. Rear-axle shaft.
37. Rear hub.
38. Wheel stud.
39. Wheel-stud nut.
40. Axle shaft to hub gasket.
41. Rear-hub oil seal.
42. Rear-hub bearing.
43. Bearing spacer.
44. Lock-nut,
45. Lock-nut tab washer.
46. Brake drum.
47. Brake-drum and axle-shaft screw.
48. Tubular shaft assembly.
49. Flange yoke.
50. Sleeve assembly yoke.
51. Kit set journal and needle.
52. Bearing assembly.
53. Journal gasket.
54. Gasket retainer.
55. Circlip.
56. Journal lubricator.
57. Rear-bolt shaft-flange yoke.
58. Bolt nut.

The clock gauge is now used to measure the depth of the pinion head in the casing. If a minus reading is given, *add* the amount shown on the gauge to the marking on the pinion head, which will give a minus result, and *reduce* the washer thickness by this amount. If a plus reading is given by the gauge, and the amount is less than the marking on the pinion head, then *reduce* the thickness of the washer by the difference between the two. If a plus reading is given and it is greater than the marking on the pinion, then *increase* the washer thickness by the difference between the two.

A washer of the thickness that has been calculated can be fitted to the pinion head and the pinion assembled with all its parts and shims totalling about 0·008 in. Tighten the driving flange nut to 140 lb.–ft., checking during tightening to ensure that the pre-load does not exceed 13 lb.–in. The correct pre-load is 11 to 13 lb.–in. and after the flange nut is correctly tightened, if the pre-load is too high the shims must be increased, whereas if it is too low they must be decreased. When the correct pre-load is achieved, the pinion can be assembled and everything tightened as no more adjustments are necessary to it.

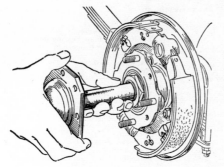

FIG. 77.—WITHDRAWING A
HALF-SHAFT FROM A MAG-
NETTE REAR AXLE, THUS
EXPOSING THE HUB-
SECURING NUT

The setting of the differential cage in the carrier is by shims
between the carrier-bearing faces and the carrier housing. The
cage is situated in the carrier and the caps tightened down to
65 lb.–ft. torque, when the clock gauge is attached to the
carrier and the backlash measured. The correct amount of
backlash should be between 0·004 and 0·007 in., but the
exact figure for the crownwheel in question is marked on its
rear face. If shims to the thickness of 0·002 in. are moved from
one side of the cage to the other, it will alter the backlash
approximately 0·002 in.

Although the above procedure is the same for all cars using
a hypoid three-quarter floating axle, naturally figures for pre-
load and backlash differ between models. The figures given
above as an example are for the 948 c.c. Midget.

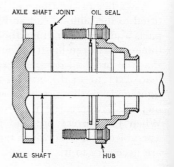

FIG. 78.—SHOWING POSITION OF THE
ADDITIONAL REAR-HUB OIL SEAL FITTED
TO B.M.C. REAR AXLES FROM MGA
AND LATER MAGNETTE ZA MODELS
ONWARDS

Reconditioned Units

With this type of axle, a reconditioned-differential unit scheme is operated by B.M.C. Service. If an owner does not wish to get involved in the rather technical operation of setting-up his differential, the old carrier assembly can simply be removed from the axle case as already described and a reconditioned unit, with all new parts and bearings and ready adjusted, can be fitted in its place.

The displaced assembly must, of course, be returned to the dealer from whom the reconditioned unit was purchased before the exchange-unit price is allowed.

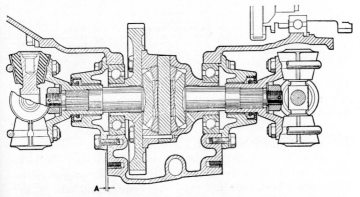

FIG. 79.—SECTION THROUGH DIFFERENTIAL OF FRONT-WHEEL DRIVE 1100 To obtain the correct preload on the differential bearings, take a feeler-gauge measurement at *A* as described in the text.

1100 Final-drive Unit

On this model there is no rear-axle assembly, instead the differential gears are placed inside the transmission unit, allowance being made at the rear of the transmission case for the fitting of a differential case, or final-drive unit.

The final drive can only be split from the transmission when it is out of the car. This is accomplished by dismantling the gear change, undoing the securing nuts and drawing off the two drive-shaft flanges, and taking out the five bolts holding the two final-drive end covers. Note the number of shims

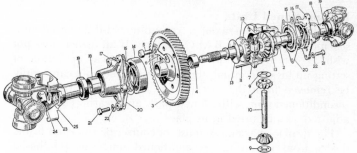

FIG. 80.—EXPLODED VIEW OF 1100 DIFFERENTIAL ASSEMBLY

1. Differential case.
2. Case bush.
3. Drive gear.
4. Gear bush.
5. Gear bolt.
6. Lock washer.
7. Thrust block.
8. Differential pinion.
9. Pinion thrust washer.
10. Centre pin.
11. Pin peg.
12. Differential gear.
13. Gear thrust washer.
14. Drive gear bearing.
15. Case bearing.
16. Bearing shim.
17. End cover.
18. Cover bush.
19. Oil seal.
20. Cover joint.
21. End cover screw.
22. Washer.
23. Driving flange.
24. Flange nut.
25. Washer.

between this and the differential bearings as they come off. The nuts securing the final-drive casing to the transmission can be taken off and the differential drawn away.

Dismantling Differential

Pull off the two differential bearings, knock back the lock-washer and remove the six bolts holding the drive gear to the cage. Mark both gear and cage for assembly and take off the gear. One differential gear and its thrust washer can now be removed from the bore of the driving gear; by tapping out the taper pin, the other differential gear and pinions can be removed from the cage.

Reassembling Differential

When reassembling, which is the reverse of the dismantling procedure, make sure that the differential-gear thrust washers are fitted with their slightly chamfered bores against the machined face of the differential gears. All parts must go back in their original positions and only the correct B.M.C. gaskets should be used. Should other makes of gaskets be fitted, it may affect the meshing of the gears, both on the final drive and the gear train down from the crankshaft.

To refit the differential, place the assembly in its housing with a slight bias towards the flywheel end of the engine. Replace the differential housing to the transmission casing with the correct gasket and tighten it enough to hold the bearings firmly, but still allow them to be moved when fitting the right-hand end cover. Attach this cover with its gasket and tighten the bolts evenly; this will move the differential assembly over. Attach the other end cover without its gasket, tightening its bolts only until the cover just nips the outer-bearing race; measure the gap between cover and casing in more than one position around its circumference. Allowing 0·007 in. for compressed thickness of the gasket, the correct gap should be 0·008–0·009 in. to give the correct pre-load of 0·001–0·002 in. Adjust by means of shims between the cover and bearing outer race and, when correct, fit the cover with its gasket and tighten its securing bolts and differential-housing bolts.

The pinion gear which drives the crownwheel is fitted on to the end of the gearbox mainshaft and has to be removed with this (see Chapter VII). There is no meshing of the crownwheel and pinion teeth other than using the correct gasket for the differential housing, as they are straight-cut gear wheels and not hypoid.

CHAPTER XI

PROPELLER SHAFT AND FRONT-WHEEL DRIVE SHAFTS

O^N all the conventional types of car covered by this book, the drive is transmitted to the rear axle via a tubular propeller shaft having at each end a Hardy Spicer universal joint. These joints are designed so that a cross-centre piece has its four ends running in needle-roller bearings, the bearing cups being fitted to the two yokes, one on the propeller shaft and the other being the flange or sliding spline, depending upon which end of the shaft is being referred to.

With the front-wheel drive 1100 there is no propeller shaft, instead two short-drive shafts run from each side of the final-drive casing out to the front hubs. At their inner ends these shafts have rubber couplings and their outer ends are fitted with constant-velocity universal joints of Birfield design.

Lubrication

Most propeller shafts have a grease nipple entering the centre of the cross piece that connects with drilled passages to lubricate the roller bearings. On the sliding spline at the front end of the shaft is a further grease nipple, but on the reverse-spline type of shaft this nipple is not fitted as lubrication of the splines takes place automatically from the rear of the gearbox. These nipples should receive attention every 3,000 miles at least.

Needle-roller Universal Joints

It is quite easy to inspect the propeller-shaft joints for signs of wear when it is in position. All that need be done is to grasp the tubular part of the shaft as close as possible to the joint and move it up and down. By watching the outer ends of the cross-

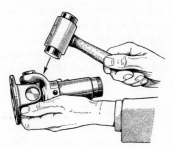

FIG. 81

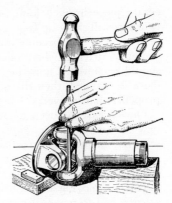

FIG. 82. — DISMANTLING UNIVERSAL
JOINT (1)

Showing where to apply light
blows to the yoke after removing the
retaining circlip.

FIG. 82

FIG. 82. — DISMANTLING UNIVERSAL
JOINT (2)

When dismantling a universal
joint the bearings may be tapped
with a small-diameter rod from the
inside.

FIG. 83

FIG. 83. — DISMANTLING UNIVERSAL
JOINT (3)

When the needle-roller bearings
have been withdrawn from opposite
sides of the spider the joint can be
separated as shown.

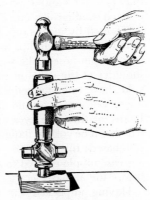

FIG. 84. — REASSEMBLING UNIVERSAL
JOINT

When replacing the gasket retainer, use should be made of a
hollow drift to tap it into place without damage.

FIG. 84

centre piece in each joint any wear between them and the bearings will show up by excess movement of the yokes.

Wear may also become noticeable during driving, for if on ordinary driving when changing from drive to over-run, should a 'clunking' noise be heard each time the direction of drive is changed, then the first thing to inspect is always the propeller-shaft universal joints.

Once wear has been diagnosed, the only remedy is to fit new cross-centre pieces and roller bearings. These are sold in sets that include the cross-centre piece, four cups and four sets of bearings for each joint on the shaft. To completely overhaul a shaft two sets are needed.

Before removing a shaft from the car, mark both the flanges at each end to make sure it is fitted in the same position and thereby not upset any balance. With the reverse-spline type of shaft only the rear end has a flange, the front is a sliding fit into the rear of the gearbox.

With the propeller shaft on the bench overhaul can commence. Clean the two joints with paraffin so that all the parts can be seen clearly, then on the sliding-joint shafts unscrew the dust cap at the rear end of the sliding joint and pull the complete universal-joint assembly off the spline shaft. Mark the two portions so they are refitted in the same positions, although there are two arrows on the parts that have to be lined up they may be missed and a second mark is helpful.

Each needle-roller cup is a taper fit in the eye of the yoke and is retained by means of a circlip. Therefore, the first job is to remove the four circlips from the yokes of the joint by using a pair of pin-nosed pliers. To get the bearing cups out, the shoulder of the yoke on the shaft, and the sides of the flange yoke, have to be tapped with a copper or lead hammer, working on one cup at a time until it is removed from the yoke eye. If any of the yoke eyes are worn or distorted then the part, whether it be yoke or flange, is scrap and a new piece has to be purchased; this, however, does not happen very often. Where a grease nipple is fitted to a cross piece it is naturally removed before the above operation takes place.

Having unpacked the new parts from the set, the cups should be taken off the cross piece, being careful to keep the needle rollers in place. Leave the oil-retaining rings on the cross piece and fit into the two yokes, then push each needle-roller cup over the cross piece, one at a time, fitting them through the yoke eyes from outside.

The needle-roller cups should be a light drive fit in the eyes and they should only be inserted far enough for the circlip to be refitted in each case. If, after all the circlips have been fitted, the joint seems to bind when it is moved in either plane, then tap the yokes gently with a copper hammer to ease the cups back hard against the circlips.

Do not forget after the propeller shaft has been refitted to lubricate the universal joints thoroughly.

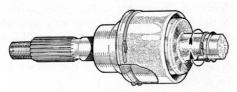

Fig. 85.—FITTING THE CONSTANT-VELOCITY-JOINT RUBBER BOOT ON A FRONT-WHEEL DRIVE SHAFT OF THE 1100

Front Drive Shafts

To remove a drive shaft from the 1100 model, the complete front swivel hub-unit has to be removed as described under Front Hubs (page 128). With the swivel hub on the bench, the split-pin and hub nut can be taken off and the splined end of the shaft drifted through the back of the hub and out.

The only purpose of removing a drive shaft will be to fit a replacement unit, as nothing can be done in the way of over-hauling the constant-velocity joint at the outer end. The joint is machined and assembled with extra care, and the Birfield Company have only recently commenced kits of parts for overhauling the joints in B.M.C. dealer workshops.

A worn drive shaft will be noticed during driving, especially when the steering is on a lock and the drive is being trans-mitted, for a sharp 'clicking' will be heard inside the car. It is possible that this is simply a lack of lubricant in the splines or joint and repacking these with the correct grease can be tried, but generally this only gives a temporary respite.

To carry out lubrication, or to fit a new rubber dirt excluder to joint or splines, the shaft has to be removed. Take off the copper wire securing the rubbers and release the small rubber from the inner end, drawing the splined part of the shaft out of the flange, then peel the large rubber off the joint.

Repack the constant-velocity joint with 1 oz. of Vaughn's ML 2 grease, available from B.M.C. dealers under part No. 97H 2612 and fit the new rubber boot, wiring it down with soft copper wire. The splined end of the shaft should be packed with $\frac{3}{4}$ oz. of special grease, B.M.C. part No. 97H 2611, and a new rubber fitted here after the flange has been replaced. Hold the lip of the rubber open as the shaft is pushed into the flange to expel any air, then check the diameter of the rubber at its bellowed part. This must not exceed $1\frac{3}{4}$ in. and if necessary squeeze it slightly to obtain this figure. Then attach the wire around the rubber to make a grease-tight seal.

The drive shaft can be refitted by reversing the removal procedure.

CHAPTER XII

BODY CARE

Fʀᴏᴍ the point of view of resale value, the bodywork of a modern car is the most important single item. Although it is not generally realised, when a car is taken in part-exchange by a garage more attention is paid to the state of the bodywork than to the mechanical parts, as they know it is far more expensive and difficult to repair the body than carry out mechanical repairs. The immediate post-war M.G. cars all used a separate body and chassis, and this continued on the sports cars until quite recently. The saloons, however, have a mono-construction body shell, that is to say there is no chassis, the mounting points for the mechanical components being part of the stressed portion of the body.

With the 1100, whilst the major mechanical units are attached to front and rear sub-frames these do not bear any great stresses, the frames are mounted to the body in such a way as to transfer stress.

Once rust is allowed to gain a good foothold on a body shell or chassis it becomes dangerous and expensive to repair. It is, therefore, most important that regular inspection of both the under and top sides of the body should be made, so that if there are any signs of rust immediate steps can be taken to clean it off. Regular body maintenance should include a weekly wash to remove all traces of mud, as this holds moisture and therefore accelerates the promotion of rust; a fortnightly or monthly wax polish as this provides a protective coating for the paintwork and the chrome parts; a regular inspection of the underside, during which the mud and other collected dirt must be washed away with a powerful hose.

Before polishing the car, inspect the paintwork and touch-up any chips or scratches with the correct coloured paint as, if these are left, rust will form and spread under the paintwork, causing it to lift and blister at a later date. Finally, it is worth-while to protect the chrome-plated parts during winter when salt and sand is used on the roads to combat ice, as these will cause the plating to deteriorate very quickly. A coating of some protective lacquer will last through the bad weather and can be cleaned off in the spring, leaving the chrome unmarked.

Hoods

Even under very good conditions there will come a time when the folding hood requires cleaning. This can be done using a mixture of pure soap and warm water, applying it by means of a soft brush. Do not use a caustic soap or spirits of any kind on the hood material, as these will give rise to damage and affect the waterproof qualities of the hood. After washing, the material should be rinsed with clean water and wiped dry with a chamois leather.

Hoods should certainly only be folded when dry, never with any water still on them, for this will get trapped in the folds and in time rot the material. Also when folding hoods make quite sure no folds of the material get trapped in the hood sticks.

Should the rear-window panel become discoloured or lightly scratched, it may be possible to improve matters by carefully rubbing with mildly abrasive metal polish and finishing with a suitable buff.

Windscreens

Unless the rubber surround has perished, the windscreen is unlikely to give any trouble. However, with the opening fold-flat screens on the sports cars, keep the hinges free and the locking nuts un-siezed, for any distortion or tightness when trying to fold a screen down can cause the glass to crack.

Water-sealing windscreens can sometimes be accomplished by using a sealing compound such as clear Bostik. Use an applicator that can give some force (something like an icing-cake gun) pulling the lip of the rubber away from the screen so the nozzle of the gun can be pushed well down before the Bostik is squeezed through. Apply the sealer to both the outer and inner lips of the rubber seal. Wipe away any compound

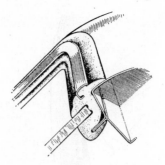

FIG. 86.—METHOD OF PULLING OUT THE CORD TO DRAW THE LIP OF THE SEAL OVER THE BODY FLANGE

FIG. 87.—SECTION THROUGH A WINDSCREEN SEALING RUBBER THAT USES A FINISHER STRIP

that is forced out as the rubber lip comes back onto the windscreen glass with a petrol-dampened rag.

If this fails to cure a leak, or if for any other reason the windscreen has to be removed, with the one-piece screens it is not too difficult a job. Generally there is a finisher, or filler, strip fitted to the centre of the rubber-screen surround; prise this out of its groove and the grip of the rubber on the screen is relaxed. Remove the interior mirror and sun visors if they are in the way and the glass can be pressed out from inside the car, starting preferably at one corner of the screen, leaving the rubber surround attached to the body aperture and this can be peeled away separately.

When refitting the glass, the body aperture should be quite clean, as should be the rubber if the same one is used. Fit the rubber to the glass and thread a length of cord around the groove that fits over the body aperture. Offer the screen up to the body and push the lower edge of the rubber over the body so that it is fitted correctly in its groove. If an assistant now pulls the cord it will come out all the way round, peeling the lip of the rubber over the body aperture. With this successfully accomplished, the filler strip can be forced into its groove to lock the rubber in position.

Different procedures are required inside the car on the

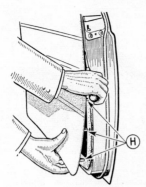

FIG. 88.—PRISING THE TRIM LINER AWAY FROM
A DOOR

The spring clips *H* can easily be levered
out of their holes in the door shell.

various models before the screen rubber can be reached. There
are sometimes finisher strips fitted to the inside windscreen
pillars, or perhaps stainless-steel finisher strips that cover the
rubber outside. All are quite easy to remove once the securing
screws or joining pieces have been taken off.

Roof Linings

Most of the roof trims on the saloon cars are fitted to a
sprung frame, the edges of the material being threaded with
galvanised wire to produce the required tension over the doors
and rear window.

The trim can generally be withdrawn towards the rear, and
as far as the door pillars or quarter-light channels as follows.
Attach a draw wire to the forward end of each side-tension
wire passing down the windscreen pillars and secure it to the
underside of the fascia by means of a self-tapping screw. Then

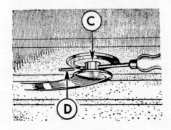

FIG. 89.—METHOD OF REMOVING INNER
DOOR HANDLES WHICH ARE SECURED
BY A PIN *D* TO LOCK SPINDLE *C*.

release the screw and compress two spring clips positioned in the roof roll behind the sun-visor locations. If it is desired to completely remove the trim, the rear-seat squab, shelf liner, quarter-trim liner and the door-pillar trim finishers must be taken off to permit the other tension-wire screws to be removed.

With the 1100, the roof lining is a foam-backed plastic material and this is attached directly to the metal underside of the roof with adhesive. To take the lining down it has to be peeled away and this cannot be done without damaging it. Therefore, removal always means a new piece of material, these being supplied already cut to the correct shape.

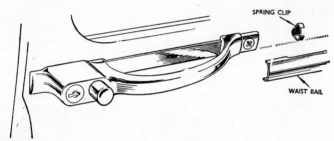

FIG. 90.—MAGNETTE ZA AND ZB OUTER DOOR HANDLE SHOWING THE FIXING SCREW COVERED BY THE WAIST RAIL

Door Locks

The removal of a door lock for attention involves, in the majority of cases, the displacement of the trim liner. This is achieved by taking off the inner-door handles and prising the trim liner away from the door shell, it being held in place by means of spring clips passing through small holes drilled in the door. If this method of attaching is not used, then the liner is probably held in place by self-tapping screws, in which case their heads will be visible around the circumference of the trim.

Before the locks can be taken out it invariably means that the door glass and window-winder mechanism have to be removed before access can be gained to the lock-securing bolts. On some of the sports-car models, the inner-door lock is in an exposed position and in any case there is no winder to bother with.

Door Glasses and Regulators

Normally, the windows are raised and lowered on the quadrant principle and unless the teeth have become worn or the spring fails, due to fatigue or misuse, a quadrant regulator is unlikely to give any trouble. Should, however, the mechanism fail to operate properly, the window glass should be removed and the complete winder assembly taken out by disconnecting it from the door shell and releasing its operating arm from the lift channel that runs along the bottom of the glass.

CHAPTER XIII

ELECTRICAL SYSTEM

THE heart of the car electrical system is the battery, this being simply a storage compartment for electricity, and it comprises a series of cells each of which provides a voltage of 2v between its two sets of plates. The cells are fitted into a battery case, three of them being used to make a 6V battery and six to make a 12V battery.

Battery Maintenance

At regular intervals, the battery vent plugs, or in the case of newer designed batteries the combined vent lid, should be removed so that the level of electrolyte in each cell can be checked. Add distilled water—*not* tap water—until the level reaches the top of the separators; do not overfill the cells as the acid might spill out and cause damage to the battery casing, as well as attacking the paint in the adjacent area.

Another warning when inspecting electrolyte levels, do not hold a naked flame near the vent holes or the gas coming off the plates may ignite. With the levels checked make sure the vent-plug holes are clear and replace the plugs, wiping the top of the battery clean and dry.

The battery terminals should also be checked periodically to make sure they are tight and not corroded. Should they need cleaning, this is easily accomplished and when refitting them it is a good idea to smear the terminal and its post with petroleum jelly.

Should the battery have to be stored for any length of time, it must be fully charged and then given a boost charge about every two weeks. It must never be allowed to stand for long periods in an uncharged condition as this will cause damage to the plates; neither must a battery be stored in a dry state after it has been charged as this will also damage it. Checks can be

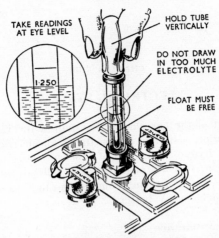

TAKE READINGS
AT EYE LEVEL

HOLD TUBE
VERTICALLY

DO NOT DRAW
IN TOO MUCH
ELECTROLYTE

1·250

FLOAT MUST
BE FREE

FIG. 91.—MEASURING SPECIFIC GRAVITY WITH A HYDROMETER

made on the specific gravity of the battery electrolyte to ascertain its condition. A hydrometer is required for this operation and the readings are as follows: fully-charged battery 1·27–1·29; half-charged battery 1·19–1·21; discharged battery 1·11–1·13.

The specific-gravity readings must never be taken immediately after topping up the electrolyte as time must be allowed for the new distilled water to thoroughly mix in.

Dynamo

This unit generates electricity as the car is being driven, feeding it to the battery at a controlled rate and thereby keeping it fully charged. All dynamos are of the two-brush type; some early models incorporate inspection ports in the casing, but on later models the windowless-yoke type is used.

In many cases, low dynamo output can be traced to slipping or broken fan belt. To adjust the fan belt, slacken the mounting bolts on the dynamo and pull this unit away from the engine, thereby making the belt tighter.

When carrying out this operation do not make the belt too tight or it will throw undue strain on the dynamo bearings. The tension should be such that there is about $\frac{3}{4}$–1 in. of

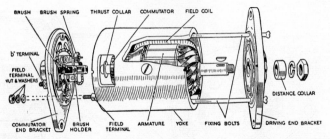

FIG. 92.—EXPLODED VIEW OF DYNAMO WITH INSPECTION WINDOW IN YOKE FOR EXAMINING BRUSHES

movement on the longest side of the belt. If this adjustment does not improve matters, then the commutator and brushes must be checked.

Remove the cover band from dynamos with inspection ports (the windowless yoke units have to be taken from the car completely as described later) and press the brushes down on to the commutator as it is possible they are sticking in their holders. If the brushes are worn down to their last $\frac{1}{4}$ in. and do not bear on to the commutator, renew them. This is achieved by lifting up the brush spring, pulling out the old brush and disconnecting its wire, and fitting the new brush in its place. Check that these brushes do not stick in their holders and if they do they should have their sides relieved slightly with a fine file.

With the windowless-yoke dynamo it can be removed from

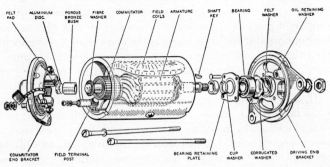

FIG. 93.—EXPLODED VIEW OF WINDOWLESS YOKE-TYPE DYNAMO

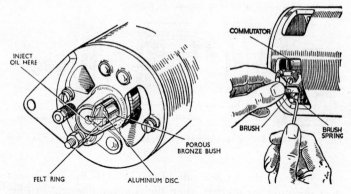

FIG. 94 (*left*).—CUTAWAY VIEW OF DYNAMO-BUSH LUBRICATOR
FIG. 95 (*right*).—CHECKING DYNAMO BRUSHES ARE FREE IN THEIR HOLDERS AND
THE SPRINGS ARE NOT WEAK

the engine by taking off the fan belt and undoing the three mounting bolts that hold it in place. Access to the brushes on this unit is gained as follows: remove the drive pulley and the Woodruff key from the shaft. Unscrew the two long bolts that pass right through the dynamo case and the back-end plate, which carries the brush gear (see Fig. 93), can be taken off. Apply the same checks as already described for the brushes, their holders and springs.

Having either proved or disproved any fault with the brushes, the commutator is the next item to be looked at. In some cases it may only be dirty and it can easily be cleaned by dipping a piece of rag in some petrol and holding this against the commutator with one hand as the drive shaft is turned with the other. If score marks or burns are present on the commutator, it requires skimming on a lathe and the mica grooves undercut; this job being best left to a dealer.

If, after making all the above checks is of no avail, the wiring must be checked. Remove, clean and refit all terminals; look closely for breaks in wiring insulation and if any are found fit new pieces of wire. Further tests on the dynamo can only be accomplished by using a moving-coil voltmeter with the dynamo being driven on the car. While very few owners will have one of these, some may be in a position to borrow one so the readings are given below.

Clip the negative lead of the voltmeter to the dynamo terminal and the other lead to a good earthing point on the dynamo yoke; start the engine and increase the speed slowly until about 1,000 r.p.m. is reached, when the voltmeter reading should increase quite rapidly, but without fluctuation. Do not allow the voltmeter reading to pass 20 volts and do not race the engine to try and increase the voltage. If no reading at all is given on the meter, check the brush gear (if this has not already been carried out). If a very low reading of about 1 volt is given, the fault is most probably in the field winding, while a reading of about 5 volts indicates a faulty armature winding. Should the latter two faults be found, the fitting of a complete exchange unit might be the best solution, the alternative being to get a rewind firm to attend to whichever winding is at fault. Should all dynamo checks give the right readings, the control box must be looked into.

Starter

Should the starter motor refuse to turn the engine and the battery is known to be fully charged, then a test must be made to ascertain the fault. Switch on the headlamps and operate the starter switch again; if the lamps immediately go dim it shows that current is passing through to the starter, but it is siezed in some way, most probably by the pinion being jammed in mesh with the flywheel ring gear. If this is the case, the starter must be removed and the pinion and its splines thoroughly cleaned and freed off.

If the lamps do not lose any brilliance when the starter switch is operated, then all the wiring, terminals, starter switch and battery connections must be checked. If these are all in order, then remove the starter-inspection port cover (if one is fitted, if not remove the starter and take off the end cover) and carry out the same checks to the brushes and commutator as listed under Dynamo. The units are very much alike in basic design. Should these checks make no difference, then an internal fault is indicated and an exchange unit is required. When cleaning a starter commutator, skimming on a

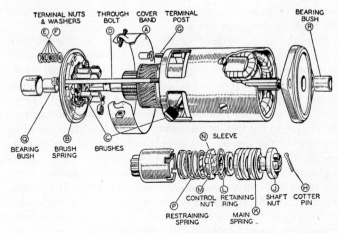

FIG. 96.—COMPONENT PARTS OF A TYPICAL STARTER MOTOR

lathe should be avoided if possible, but if it has to be done, take as fine a cut as possible and do *not* undercut the mica between the segments as is done with a dynamo.

One other occurrence that sometimes comes to light is a slow turning or sluggish starter. Again, if the battery is known to be in good condition a wiring check must be made as a poor connection in the circuit produces a high resistance. Also faulty or worn brushes might be to blame.

To remove a starter pinion that is tight or worn, the starter must be taken off the engine and placed on the bench. Withdraw the split-pin from the nut on the end of the shaft and by holding the squared end of the starter shaft, unscrew the nut. Lift off the main spring and remove the retaining ring, when the control nut, spring and sleeve will slide off the shaft. Withdraw the splined washer and the pinion can be taken off. Replacement is opposite to this and Fig. 161 shows all the components in their correct order.

Fuses

On some cars, the fuses are situated under the control box and are marked 'AUX' and 'AUX IGN', whereas other models have a separate fuse box and the fuses are marked 'A1–A2' and 'A3–A4'.

The 'AUX' or the 'A1–A2' fuses on respective models protect the accessories which are wired so that they operate regardless as to whether the ignition switch is on or off. Those marked 'AUX IGN' and 'A3–A4' protect the accessories which only operate when the ignition is switched on. By referring to the wiring diagrams it can be seen which units are protected by which fuses. Accessories in the above context includes units such as windscreen wipers, trafficators, lights, etc., as well as additional fitments that have been placed on the car by the owner.

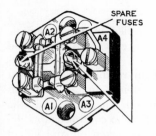
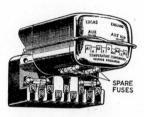

Fig. 97.—TWO TYPES OF FUSE BOX FITTED TO VARIOUS MODELS

If any of the accessories covered by the fuses fail to operate, the first check is always at the respective fuse. If it has blown this can easily be seen through the glass-tubed centre as the wire will be broken. Before fitting a new fuse a check should be made to see if there is a wiring fault in the units concerned that caused the fuse to blow.

Control Box

The control box is a housing for two units—a voltage regulator and a cut-out. Although in the same basic box, so to speak, these two units are completely separate electrically.

The Regulator

The regulator is set to maintain dynamo output between close pre-determined limits at all speeds above regulating

F

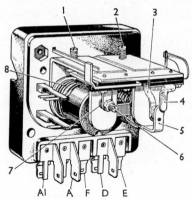

Fig. 98.—CONTROL BOX USED ON MODELS FROM 1965 ONWARDS

1. Regulator adjusting screw.
2. Cut-out adjusting screw.
3. Fixed contact blade.
4. Stop arm.
5. Armature tongue and moving contact.
6. Regulator fixed-contact screw.
7. Regulator moving contact.
8. Regulator series windings.

point, the field strength being controlled by the automatic insertion and withdrawal of a resistance in the dynamo field circuit.

Adjustment of the regulator again requires the use of a moving-coil voltmeter, this unit having one of its leads attached to the control-box terminal D (negative lead) the other being connected to terminal E. The control-box cables on the terminals A and A1 should be taken off and joined together.

Start the engine and slowly increase its speed until the voltmeter needle flickers then steadies, this should occur at a reading of between 15·8 and 16·7 volts, according to the temperature. If the voltage at which the needle steadies is outside these limits then the adjusting screw must be turned clockwise to raise the setting or anti-clockwise to lower it until the voltmeter reading comes right. Only turn the adjusting screw a fraction at a time.

The Cut-out.—The cut-out is an electro-magnetically-operated switch connected to the charging circuit between the dynamo and the battery. It automatically connects the dynamo to the battery when dynamo output exceeds that of the battery and disconnects the two when the dynamo output falls.

For adjustments, take the moving-coil voltmeter and connect it to terminals D and E on the control box, then start the

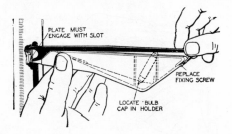

FIG. 99.—RENEWING A
TRAFFICATOR BULB

PLATE MUST
ENGAGE WITH SLOT

REPLACE
FIXING SCREW

LOCATE BULB
CAP IN HOLDER

engine and slowly increase its speed until the cut-out contacts are seen to close, noting the voltage at which this occurs. It should be 12·7–13·3 volts.

If the cut-out operates outside these limits, the adjusting screw should be turned clockwise to raise the voltage setting, or anti-clockwise to reduce the setting. Check the reading after each movement of the adjusting screw and make the adjustments as quickly as possible to avoid possible damage due to temperature rise.

Trafficators

Fitting of new bulbs to trafficator arms is quite easy, all that need be done is for the arm to be lifted out of its socket and the small screw removed from the end of the metal cover. The plastic arm can then be pulled down from the cover far enough to lift out the bulb and insert a new one. It is important that before the arm is lifted, the ignition is switched on and the trafficator switch operated for the side to be worked upon. Do not try to prise out an arm with the switch not being operated.

Should a trafficator arm fail to raise in response to the switch, it may just require a drop of light oil on the arm pivot. Should this not cure the fault, make a check on the feed wire to the unit, the fuse that covers the circuit, clean all the terminals and try again. If the arm still refuses to rise, then there is probably an internal fault and an exchange unit is the best answer.

Flashing Indicators

The flashing indicators require no maintenance and the only thing that can cause them to fail is a blown fuse, a blown bulb

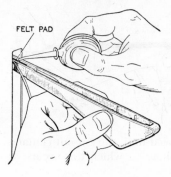

FIG. 100 (*left*).—LUBRICATING FELT PAD IN TRAFFICATOR ARM

FIG. 101 (*below*).—LUBRICATING TRAFFICATOR-ARM BEARING

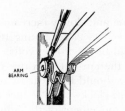

or a faulty flasher unit. This is of aluminium which is generally mounted under the bonnet on the bulkhead, with three terminals coming from its top; it can be replaced simply by undoing its mounting screws and pulling off the wire connectors, joining them to the new unit in exactly the same positions.

Should the wiring ever prove to be faulty, the positions of all the wires concerned with the circuit can be found in the relevant wiring diagram.

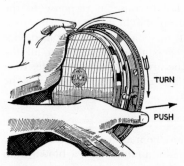

FIG. 102.—REMOVING HEADLAMP UNIT

Lighting

Outer lamp lens are fitted in a variety of ways depending upon the model; there is sometimes a chrome surround with one or two screws, or a chrome rim that fits into a rubber lip, while on occasions the lens itself fits inside a rubber lip.

Headlamp units are held in place by a rim with a screw passing through the underside. To take out a headlamp unit, remove the rim and press in the lamp unit against its spring pressure, turn it clockwise and the unit will come off its adjusting screws. Bulbs are fitted into holders that clip into the rear of the reflector unit. Side- and tail-lamp bulbs are normal bayonet types, fitting into holders.

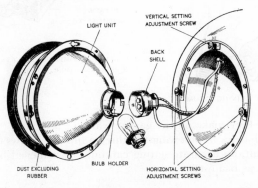

FIG. 103.—THE MOST COMMON TYPE OF BULB HOLDER
FOR HEADLAMPS

On some of the latest models sealed-beam headlamps are fitted, these being complete lens/reflector/bulb units with no separate bulbs that can be renewed. When one fails, a complete light unit has to be part exchanged for a new one.

All drivers who travel a lot at night realise the importance of correct beam-setting and will no doubt agree that bad accidents can occur because of headlamps being wrongly adjusted. For this reason periodic checks on the positions of the headlamp beams should be made at a garage having the necessary equipment. It is not really advisable for owners to try and adjust their own headlamps by seeing what kind of

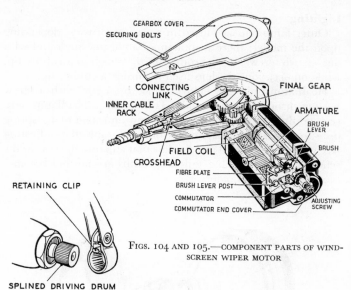

FIGS. 104 AND 105.—COMPONENT PARTS OF WIND-
SCREEN WIPER MOTOR

pattern they make on the garage wall, for although they can
make changes by screwing the three adjusting screws on each
light unit, an accurate setting can only be achieved by using
the Lucas Beamsetter.

Windscreen Wipers

The motor for the windscreen wipers is generally mounted
on the bulkhead under the bonnet, the driving cable passing
through the double skin of the bulkhead to drive the two
wiper-blade spindles. The only maintenance that is required
by the wipers is an occasional changing of the rubber blades;
this should be carried out as soon as they wear to such an
extent that they fail to clear the screen properly.

Should the wipers fail to work, always check the wiring, fuse
and connections before turning to the motor itself. If this
makes no improvement, remove the top cover from the motor
and clean, if required, the commutator. Should the brushes be
worn or not running on the commutator, renew them,
together with new tension springs.

When a wiper motor wears out its brushes and commutator, it is generally also so badly worn in other respects (i.e. bearings, windings, shafts etc.) that the best course of action is to fit a reconditioned unit.

Conclusion

While it is possible for most owners to change such things as gauges and switches and fit new wiring, the main difficulty is checking the unit concerned to ascertain whether or not it is faulty.

The only way to do this is by replacement of the suspected unit, and many garages are reluctant to let owners have parts on trial in case they are damaged during fitment and then returned because the original unit was not at fault at all. It is best, therefore, to leave the diagnosing of faulty units to an M.G. dealer, who will be able to wire them to test equipment and find out if they are serviceable.

One final point to always remember, when working on the electrical system, is to disconnect the battery to avoid a short-circuit, for a big spark in the region of the carburetter could have fatal consequences.

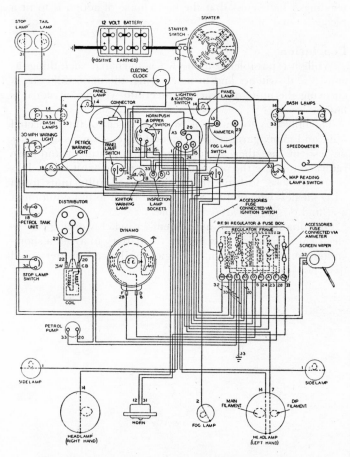

FIG. 106.—WIRING DIAGRAM FOR MIDGET SERIES TC (1945–6)
Key to cable colours is as given on page 170.

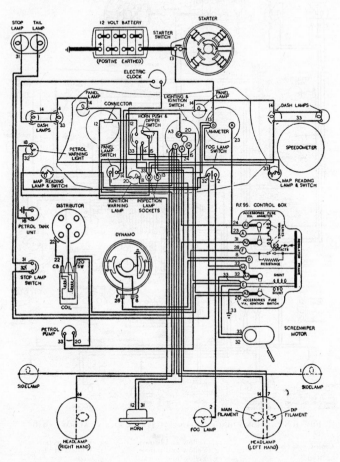

FIG. 107.—WIRING DIAGRAM FOR MIDGET SERIES TC (1947–8)
Key to cable colours is as given on page 170.

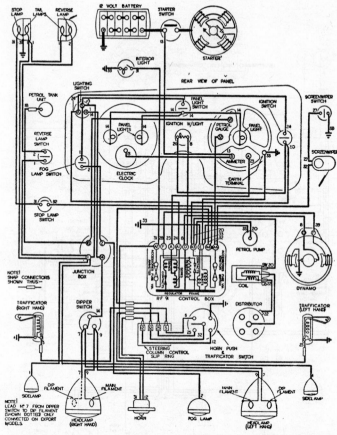

FIG. 108.—WIRING DIAGRAM FOR 1¼-LITRE SERIES Y SALOON (1946–7)

Cable Colour Code.

1. Red.	11. Yellow and brown.	23. White and purple.
2. Red and yellow.	12. Yellow and purple.	24. White and black.
3. Red and blue.	13. Yellow and black.	25. Green.
4. Red and white.	14. Blue.	26. Green and brown.
5. Red and green.	15. Blue and white.	27. Green and purple.
6. Red and brown.	16. Blue and green.	28. Green and black.
7. Red and black.	17. Blue and brown.	29. Brown.
8. Yellow.	18. Blue and purple.	30. Brown and purple.
9. Yellow and blue.	19. Blue and black.	31. Purple.
10. Yellow and green.	20. White.	32. Purple and black.
	21. White and green.	33. Black.
	22. White and brown.	

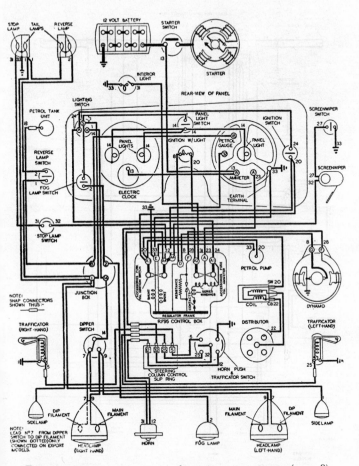

FIG. 109.—WIRING DIAGRAM FOR 1¼-LITRE SERIES Y SALOON (1947–8)

Key to cable colours is as given on page 170.

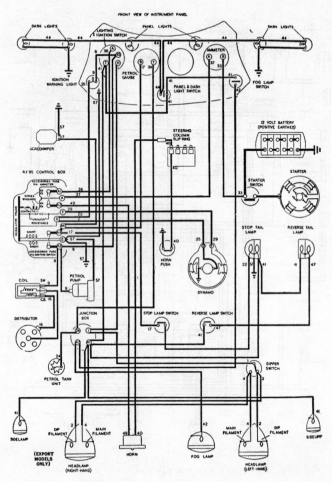

FIG. 110.—WIRING DIAGRAM FOR 1¼-LITRE SERIES Y TOURER (1949)
For key to cable colours, see page 179.

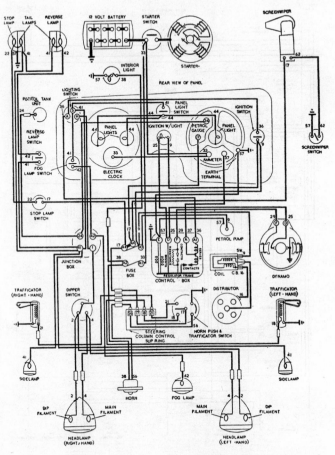

FIG. III.—WIRING DIAGRAM FOR 1¼-LITRE SERIES YB SALOON (1951–3)
For key to cable colours, see page 179.

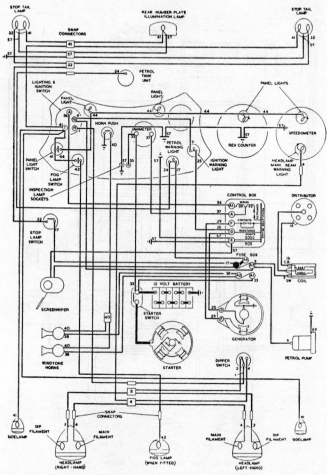

FIG. 112.—WIRING DIAGRAM FOR MIDGET SERIES TD (1953)
For key to cable colours, see page 179.

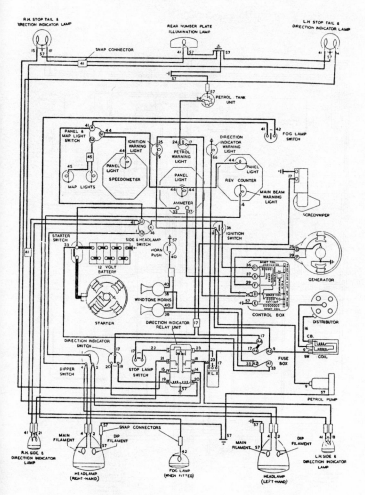

FIG. 113.—WIRING DIAGRAM FOR MIDGET SERIES TF (1953)
For key to cable colours, see page 179.

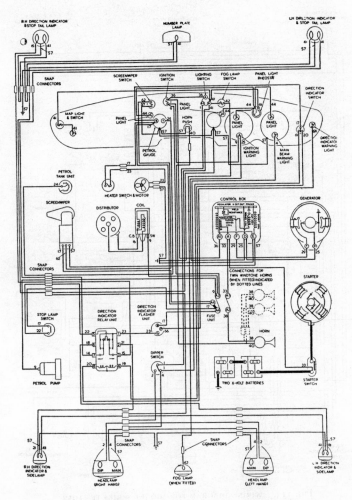

FIG. 114.—WIRING DIAGRAM FOR MGA 1500 (1955-9)
For key to cable colours, see page 179.

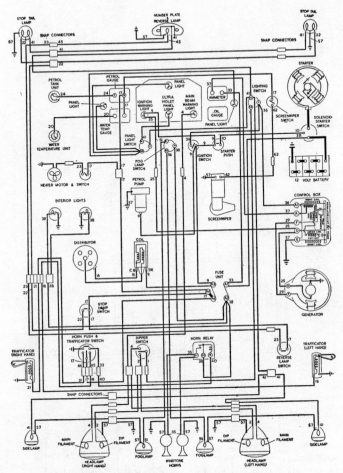

FIG. 115.—WIRING DIAGRAM FOR MAGNETTE (1954-7)

For key to cable colours, see page 179.

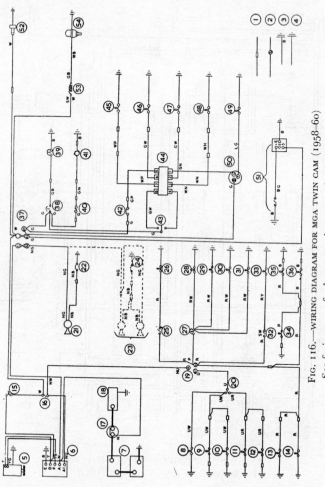

FIG. 116.—WIRING DIAGRAM FOR MGA TWIN CAM (1958—60)

See facing page for key to equipment and colour code.

CABLE COLOUR CODE FOR FIGS. 110–115 AND 117

1. Blue.	23. Green with brown.	45. Red with green.
2. Blue with red.	24. Green with black.	46. Red with purple.
3. Blue with yellow.	25. Yellow.	47. Red with brown.
4. Blue with white.	26. Yellow with red.	48. Red with black.
5. Blue with green.	27. Yellow with blue.	49. Purple.
6. Blue with purple.	28. Yellow with white.	50. Purple with red.
7. Blue with brown.	29. Yellow with green.	51. Purple with yellow.
8. Blue with black.	30. Yellow with purple.	52. Purple with blue.
9. White.	31. Yellow with brown.	53. Purple with white.
10. White with red.	32. Yellow with black.	54. Purple with green.
11. White with yellow.	33. Brown.	55. Purple with brown.
12. White with blue.	34. Brown with red.	56. Purple with black.
13. White with green.	35. Brown with yellow.	57. Black.
14. White with purple.	36. Brown with blue.	58. Black with red.
15. White with brown.	37. Brown with white.	59. Black with yellow
16. White with black.	38. Brown with green.	60. Black with blue.
17. Green.	39. Brown with purple.	61. Black with white.
18. Green with red.	40. Brown with black.	62. Black with green.
19. Green with yellow.	41. Red.	63. Black with purple.
20. Green with blue.	42. Red with yellow.	64. Black with brown.
21. Green with white.	43. Red with blue.	65. Dark green.
22. Green with purple.	44. Red with white.	66. Light green.

KEY TO EQUIPMENT FOR MGA TWIN CAM

1. Snap connectors.	15. Ignition warning light.	36. Number-plate lamp.
2. Terminal blocks or junction box.	16. Ignition switch.	37. Fuse block.
	17. Starter switch.	38. Fuel gauge.
3. Earth connections made via cable.	18. Starter motor.	39. Fuel tank unit.
	19. Lighting switch.	40. Heater switch.
4. Earth connections made via fixing bolt.	20. Dipper switch.	41. Heater motor.
	21. Single horn (standard).	42. Stop lamp switch.
5. Generator.	22. Horn-push.	43. Flasher switch.
6. Control box.	23. Twin horns (optional extra).	44. Relay.
7. Two 6-volt batteries.		45. Left-hand rear flasher and stop lamp.
8. Main beam warning light.	24. Horn-push.	46. Left-hand front flasher.
	25. Map lamp switch.	47. Right-hand front flasher.
9. Right-hand headlamp main beam.	26. Map lamp.	48. Right-hand rear flasher and stop lamp.
	27. Panel light rheostat.	
10. Left-hand headlamp main beam.	28. Panel light.	49. Flasher warning light.
	29. Panel light.	50. Flasher unit.
11. Right-hand headlamp dip beam.	30. Panel light.	51. Screen wiper switch and motor.
	31. Panel light.	
12. Left-hand headlamp dip beam.	32. Fog lamp switch.	52. Fuel pump.
	33. Fog lamp.	53. Ignition coil.
13. Left-hand sidelamp.	34. Left-hand tail lamp.	54. Distributor.
14. Right-hand sidelamp.	35. Right-hand tail lamp.	

CABLE COLOUR CODE FOR FIGS 116, 118–123

B Black.	P Purple.	Y Yellow.
U Blue.	R Red.	D Dark.
N Brown.	S Slate.	L Light.
G Green	W White	M Medium
K Pink.		

When a cable has two colour code letters, the first denotes the main colour and the second denotes the tracer colour.

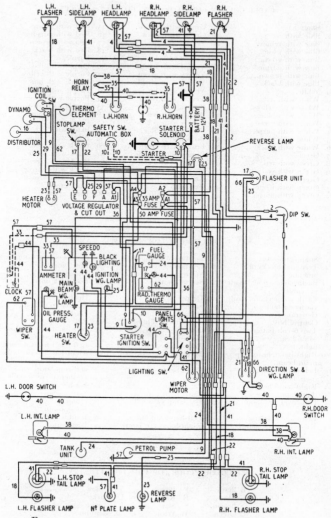

FIG. 117.—WIRING DIAGRAM FOR MAGNETTE MARK III (1959–60)

For key to cable colours, see page 179.

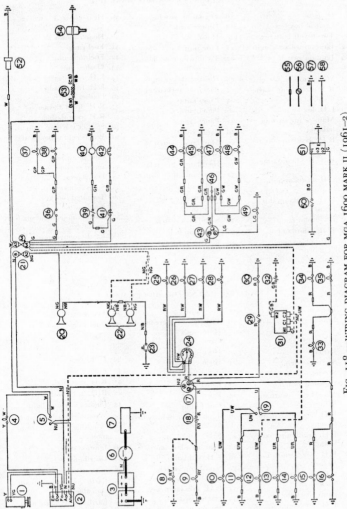

FIG. 118.—WIRING DIAGRAM FOR MGA 1600 MARK II (1961–2)

For key to cable colours, see page 179; key to equipment is given on page 182.

KEY TO EQUIPMENT FOR MGA MARK II

1. Dynamo.
2. Control box.
3. Two 6-volt batteries.
4. Ignition warning light.
5. Ignition switch.
6. Starter switch.
7. Starter motor.
8. R.H. fog lamp (where fitted).
9. L.H. fog lamp
10. Main-beam warning light.
11. R.H. headlamp main beam.
12. L.H. headlamp main beam.
13. L.H. headlamp dip beam.
14. R.H. headlamp dip beam.
15. L.H. pilot lamp.
16. R.H. pilot lamp
17. Lighting switch.
18. Fog-lamp switch.
19. Dipper switch.
20. Horn.
21. Fuse unit.
22. Twin windtone horns (where fitted).
23. Horn-push.
24. Panel-lamp rheostat.
25. Panel lamp.
26. Panel lamp.
27. Panel lamp.
28. Panel lamp.
29. Map-lamp switch.
30. Map lamp.
31. Headlamp flick relay.
32. Headlamp flick switch.
33. L.H. tail lamp.
34. Number-plate lamp.
35. R.H. tail lamp.
36. Stop-lamp switch.
37. L.H. stop lamp.
38. R.H. stop lamp.
39. Heater switch (where fitted).
40. Heater motor.
41. Fuel gauge.
42. Fuel-tank unit.
43. Flasher unit.
44. L.H. rear flasher.
45. L.H. front flasher.
46. Flasher switch.
47. R.H. front flasher.
48. R.H. rear flasher.
49. Flasher warning light.
50. Windshield wiper switch.
51. Windshield wiper motor.
52. Fuel pump.
53. Ignition coil.
54. Distributor.
55. Snap connectors.
56. Terminal blocks or junction box.
57. Earth connections made via cable.
58. Earth connections made via fixing bolts.

KEY TO EQUIPMENT FOR MIDGET MARK I

1. Dynamo.
2. Ignition-warning light.
3. Ignition switch.
4. Control box.
5. Battery.
6. Starter switch.
7. Starter motor.
8. Lighting switch.
9. Main-beam warning light.
10. R.H. headlamp main beam.
11. L.H. headlamp main beam.
12. R.H. headlamp dip beam.
13. L.H. headlamp dip beam.
14. Dipper switch.
15. L.H. sidelamp.
16. R.H. sidelamp.
17. Fuse unit.
18. Twin horn (where fitted).
19. Horn-push (where fitted).
20. Horn-push.
21. Horn.
22. Panel light switch.
23. Panel light.
24. Panel light.
25. Panel light.
26. Tachometer light (where fitted).
27. R.H. tail lamp.
28. Number-plate lamp.
29. L.H. tail lamp.
30. Stop-lamp switch.
31. L.H. stop lamp.
32. R.H. stop lamp.
33. Heater switch.
34. Heater motor (where fitted).
35. Fuel gauge.
36. Fuel-gauge tank unit.
37. Flasher unit.
38. L.H. front flasher.
39. L.H. rear flasher.
40. Flasher switch.
41. R.H. rear flasher.
42. R.H. front flasher.
43. Flasher-warning light.
44. Windshield-wiper switch.
45. Windshield-wiper motor.
46. Ignition coil.
47. Distributor.
48. Snap connectors.
49. Earth connections made via cable.
50. Earth connections made via fixing bolts.

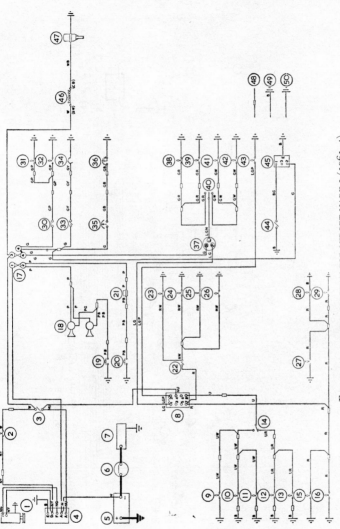

Fig. 119.—WIRING DIAGRAM FOR MIDGET MARK I (1961–4)

For key to cable colours, see page 179; key to equipment is given on facing page.

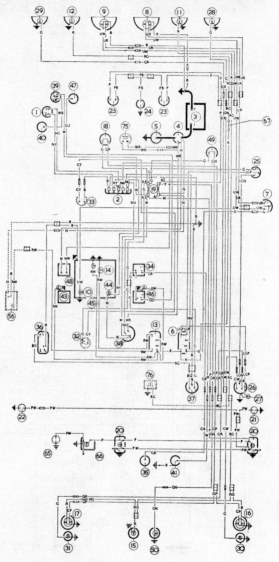

FIG. 120.—WIRING DIAGRAM FOR MAGNETTE MARK IV (FROM 1961)

For key to cable colours, see page 179; key to equipment is given on page 186.

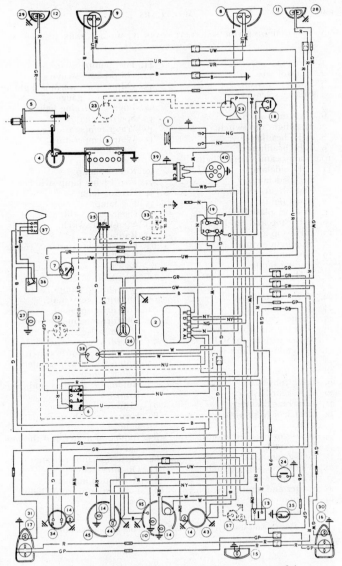

FIG. 121.—WIRING DIAGRAM FOR MIDGET MARK II (FROM 1964)

For key to cable colours, see page 179; key to equipment is given on page 186.

KEY TO EQUIPMENT FOR MAGNETTE MARK IV, MIDGET MARK II, 1100, MGB
AND MGB GT

1. Dynamo.
2. Control box.
3. Battery (12-volt).
4. Starter solenoid.
5. Starter motor.
6. Lighting switch.
7. Headlight dip switch.
8. R.H. headlamp.
9. L.H. headlamp.
10. Main-beam warning light.
11. R.H. sidelamp.
12. L.H. sidelamp.
13. Panel lights switch.
14. Panel lights.
15. Number-plate lamp.
16. R.H. stop and tail lamp.
17. L.H. stop and tail lamp.
18. Stop light switch.
19. Fuse unit (35 amps.).
20. Interior lamp.
21. R.H. door switch.
22. L.H. door switch.
23. Horn (twin horns).
24. Horn push.
25. Flasher unit.
26. Direction-indicator switch and flasher switch on MGB).
27. Direction-indicator warning lights.
28. R.H. front flasher.
29. L.H. front flasher.
30. R.H. rear flasher.
31. L.H. rear flasher.
32. Heater or fresh-air motor switch.
33. Heater or fresh-air motor.
34. Fuel gauge.
35. Fuel-gauge tank unit.
36. Windshield wiper switch.
37. Windshield wiper.
38. Starter and ignition switch.
39. Ignition coil.
40. Distributor.

41. Fuel pump.
42. Oil-pressure switch.
43. Oil-pressure warning light or oil-pressure gauge.
44. Ignition-warning light.
45. Speedometer.
46. Water-temperature gauge.
47. Water-temperature transmitter.
49. Reverse-lamp switch.
50. Reverse lamp.
53. Fog/driving lamp switches.
54. Driving lamp.
55. Fog lamp.
57. Cigar-lighter (illuminated).
59. Map-light switch.
60. Radio.
64. Bi-metal instrument voltage stabilizer.
65. Boot-lamp switch.
66. Boot lamp.
67. Line fuse (35 amps.).
68. Overdrive relay unit.
71. Overdrive solenoid.
72. Overdrive manual-control switch.
73. Overdrive gear switch.
74. Overdrive throttle switch.
75. Automatic gearbox safety switch.
76. Automatic gearbox indicator lamp.
81. Ashtray illumination.
82. Heater or fresh air switch light.
83. Induction heater and thermostat.
84. Suction-chamber heater.
94. Oil-filter switch.
95. Revolution indicator.
105. Lubrication warning light lead.

Note. Circuits shown dotted in wiring diagrams are optional extras.

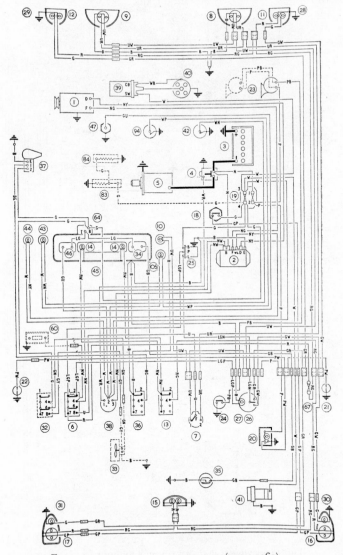

FIG. 122.—WIRING DIAGRAM FOR 1100 (FROM 1962)

For key to cable colours, see page 179; key to equipment is given on facing page.

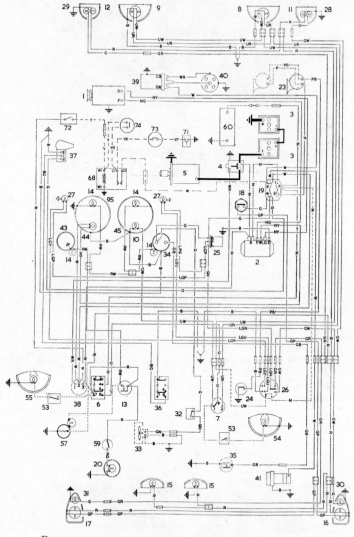

FIG. 123.—WIRING DIAGRAM FOR MGB AND MGB GT (FROM 1962)

For key to cable colours, see page 179; key to equipment is given on page 186.

INDEX